The
Anne Boleyn
Collection

Claire Ridgway

M MadeGlobal Publishing

For more information on
MadeGlobal Publishing, visit our website:
www.madeglobal.com

To everyone who has visited
The Anne Boleyn Files over the past three years and who has
given me such support and encouragement – thank you!

To Tim, Christian, Verity & Joel for coping with
me talking about the Boleyns all the time xxxxx

To Dr. Linda Saether for the idea. Thank you!

To the Boleyns for existing!

"Le temps viendra, Je Anne Boleyn"

Author Bio

Claire Ridgway is a writer, researcher and Tudor history detective with a deep knowledge and love of everything about the Boleyn family and the time of the Tudors. She is well known and respected for her two Tudor websites **www.theanneboleynfiles.com** and **www.elizabethfiles.com** which contain in-depth research about the period and which promote historical authenticity. Claire is also active in running an exclusive members website with all of the latest research about Anne Boleyn and her family.

Claire currently lives up a mountain in Southern Spain, but grew up near to Stratford-upon-Avon where she was surrounded by Tudor history. Claire is Tudor obsessed, and makes no apologies for it.

Praise for The Anne Boleyn Files

"The Anne Boleyn Files is a daily must-read for me. Here's the real Anne Boleyn, all the history, passion and mystery of her life plus a lively community of history fans. Warning: it's addictive."
Jeane Westin - His Last Letter

"The Anne Boleyn Files has been of immense value to me. I simply LOVE it!"
Anne Barnhill - At the Mercy of the Queen

"The Anne Boleyn Files is a unique one-stop delight chock full of engaging articles, little-known tidbits, and thoughtful editorials that always find a fresh, but authentic, angle. Any Anne fan can happily click away hours each week at the site and never fail to find a useful or thrilling fact or insight."
Sandra Byrd, best-selling author of
To Die For: A Novel of Anne Boleyn

Contents

Introduction 1

Did Anne Boleyn Have Six Fingers? 3

Anne Boleyn and The Other Boleyn Girl. 7

"The Tudors" – Is it Really So Bad? 17

The Six Wives' Stereotypes. 19

Catherine of Aragon – The Boring One? 21

Anne Boleyn – The Mysterious and Maligned One 33

Jane Seymour: The Meek and Mild One? 47

Anne of Cleves – Flanders Mare? 59

Catherine Howard – The Material Girl? 67

Catherine Parr – The Old Nursemaid? 83

Should Anne Boleyn be Pardoned and Reburied as Queen?. . 95

The Scandalous and Corrupt Anne Boleyn? 101

The Sexualization of Anne Boleyn 105

Anne Boleyn – "The Great Whore" 109

Anne Boleyn's Remains – The Exhumation of Anne Boleyn. . 113

Anne Boleyn's Body Found? 121

Should Henry VIII be Exhumed and Would it
Provide the Answer to his Tyranny? 129

Anne Boleyn and Catherine of Aragon – Part 1. 135

Anne Boleyn and Catherine of Aragon – Part 2. 141

Did Anne Boleyn Commit Incest with Her Brother? 147

Did Anne Boleyn Dig Her Own Grave? 153

Did Henry VIII Commit Bigamy When He
Married Anne Boleyn? 157

Anne Boleyn and Henry VIII's Marriage:
Doomed from the Start? 161

Anne Boleyn's Ladies-in-Waiting 169

Anne Boleyn's Household 181

The Lost Boleyns – Thomas and Henry Boleyn 189

The Lost Boleyns – Update on the Tomb Brasses of
Thomas and Henry Boleyn 197

The Lost Boleyns – Claire's still digging! .199
George Boleyn, Lord Rochford, Part 1 201
George Boleyn, Lord Rochford, Part 2 211
George Boleyn, Lord Rochford, Part 3 219
17th May 1536 -The Deaths of 5 Men and a
Marriage Destroyed 229
19th May 1536 – I Have a Little Neck. The
Execution of Anne Boleyn 237
Anne Boleyn – All Things to All People. 239
Index 247

Introduction

On the 17th February 2009 I published my very first post on The Anne Boleyn Files website. It was entitled "In Search of the Real Anne Boleyn" and opened with the words: "My purpose in starting this blog is to record and share my journey of discovery, my mission to expose the real Anne Boleyn". When I read those words now, nearly three years on, I'm proud to say that they still ring 100% true. My purpose in running The Anne Boleyn Files is still to share my research and my discoveries, and to educate visitors about the real Anne Boleyn, the woman behind the myths.

Those of you who know me, or who have followed the site since its birth, will know that it was inspired by a dream I had in January 2009. I can't remember much about that dream now, but it really shook me up and had a major impact on me at the time. All I can remember is that I was a member of the crowd at Anne Boleyn's execution on the 19th May 1536 and I knew that she was innocent of the charges that she had been found guilty of. I was paralysed, rooted to the spot and my mouth was like sandpaper, I couldn't utter a word. I was completely helpless. I woke up in a cold sweat just as the executioner swung the sword to behead Anne and woke my husband, Tim, to tell him that he had to design a website for me called The Anne Boleyn Files because I had to tell Anne's story.

Now, that all sounds like complete gobbledy-gook, doesn't it? A website set up because of a dream! What am I on?! And, no, I don't believe that Anne was reaching out to me from beyond the grave or that I was present at her execution in another life. I just believe that the website was my true vocation. At the time of my dream, I was a freelance writer writing articles, books, web content etc. for people all over the world, and I was happy to a degree but I wasn't writing about my passion. Running The Anne Boleyn Files brought together my two loves: writing and history, and I can honestly say, hand on heart, that I love every minute of my research and writing now, and I get such a buzz when I hear from people saying how much they have learned from my work.

This book is a celebration of The Anne Boleyn Files website's success and it brings together some of the most popular articles from the site. I thought it was an appropriate way to mark our 3 year anniversary. I dedicate it to everyone who visits the site on a regular basis and who has given me so much encouragement and support. I look on The Anne Boleyn Files as a community of Tudor history lovers and people who care about these characters' real stories and feel blessed to be a part of it. Thank you for making it what it is today, thank you!

Claire Ridgway

Did Anne Boleyn Have Six Fingers?

Along with blood-curdling ghost stories, tall tales and gory descriptions of botched executions, visitors to the Tower of London are sometimes told that Anne Boleyn had six fingers on one hand. Allegedly, this was proved when the Victorian team who exhumed her body found her extra finger bones. But is there any truth in this, or is it simply another tall tale?

In his book "Rise and Growth of the Anglican Schism" (1585), Catholic recusant Nicholas Sander gives a rather unflattering description of Anne Boleyn:-

"Anne Boleyn was rather tall of stature, with black hair, and an oval face of a sallow complexion, as if troubled with jaundice. She had a projecting tooth under the upper lip, and on her right hand six fingers. There was a large wen under her chin, and therefore to hide its ugliness she wore a high dress covering her throat... She was handsome to look at, with a pretty mouth, amusing in her ways, playing well on the lute, and was a good dancer."

I'm always amused by the fact that she had a jaundiced complexion, six fingers and a growth under her chin but Sander still found her "handsome to look at"!

While this passage is often given as proof that Anne Boleyn had an extra finger on one of her hands, we have to consider the author, Nicholas Sander, and how accurate his description is likely to be. We have to take into account the following:-

- That Nicholas Sander was a Catholic forced into exile by the reign of the Protestant Elizabeth I, daughter of Anne Boleyn. He was therefore rather biased!

- That he was born in around 1530 and was therefore only 6 years old when Anne Boleyn died.

- That other parts of his book are inaccurate. For example, he writes of a fifteen year old Anne Boleyn being sent to France because she "sinned first with her father's butler, and then with his chaplain". This simply could not have happened. At the age of fifteen, Anne was already in France, serving Queen Claude and had been on the Continent for three years. Sander also writes that Anne Boleyn was actually Henry VIII's daughter and that she slept with Francis I before moving on to sleeping with her father Henry VIII!

We therefore have to take Sander's description of Anne with a hefty pinch of salt.

But Sander is not the only source for the six fingers story. George Wyatt, grandson of Thomas Wyatt, the poet and courtier who was once in love with Anne Boleyn, wrote:-

"There was found, indeed, upon the side of her nail upon one of her fingers, some little show of a nail, which yet was so small, by the report of those that have seen her, as the workmaster seemed to leave it an occasion of greater grace to her hand, which, with the tip of one of her other fingers, might be and was usually by her hidden without any least blemish to it. Likewise there were said to be upon some parts of her body certain small moles incident to the clearest complexions."

This description appeared in Wyatt's biography of Anne Boleyn, "Life of Queen Anne Boleigne", which was favourable to Anne and although it was not written until the turn of the 17th century it was based on accounts of those who knew her. However, "some little show of nail" is very different to a sixth finger!

Those two sources are the only 16th century mentions of Anne Boleyn having some kind of deformity or blemish on one of her hands. Eustace Chapuys, the Imperial Ambassador, who was so hostile to Anne Boleyn that he always referred to her as "the concubine", makes no mention of any deformities or a sixth finger, yet he surely would have reported this to the Emperor with glee! Even if Anne used long sleeves to hide her hand on a daily basis, she could not have kept it hidden all the time and especially not from Henry VIII. Would a king who was paranoid about disease, curses and the succession move heaven and earth to marry a woman who had six fingers? No, I don't believe so. Moles and beauty spots he could handle but a sixth finger that could be passed on to his son and heir? No, not likely.

But what about the sixth finger that was found on Anne's hand when the Victorians dug her up? Well, this is pure fiction, a tall tale told by the entertaining Yeoman Warders at the Tower of London.

In 1876, restoration work was carried out on the Chapel of St Peter ad Vincula at the Tower of London, the resting place of three queens: Anne Boleyn, Catherine Howard and Lady Jane Grey. The work was recorded by Doyne C. Bell, who describes himself as "Secretary to Her Majesty's Privy Purse", in his book "Notices of the Historic Persons Buried in the Chapel of St Peter ad Vincula in the Tower of London, With an Account of the Discovery of the Supposed Remains of Anne Boleyn". It had been planned to leave the chancel undisturbed because it was the resting place of prominent people, including the Tudor queens. However, the surveyor noticed that the pavement was sinking and this needed correcting.

Bell used historical sources and records to make a plan of the resting places in the chancel and it was decided that any remains found should be re-interred on the same spot and labelled. When the pavement was lifted in the area thought to have been the resting place of Anne Boleyn, the bones of a female were found at a depth of about two feet, "not lying in the original order, but which had evidently for some reason or other been heaped together into a smaller space." The bones were then examined by Dr Mouat who confirmed that they belonged to "a female of between twenty-five and thirty years of age, of a delicate frame of body, and who had been of slender and perfect proportions". He went on to describe the woman, explaining that "the forehead and lower jaw were small and especially well formed. The vertebrae were particularly small, especially one joint (the atlas), which was that next to the skull, and they bore witness to the Queen's 'lyttel neck.'" Although the bones were mixed up, there were no further female remains at that spot. In a memorandum attached to the minutes of the 11th

November 1876 committee meeting, Dr Mouat shared his report on the examination of the remains, commenting that "the hands and feet bones indicate delicate and well-shaped hands and feet, with tapering fingers and a narrow foot." He had found nothing unusual on the hand bones and would certainly have mentioned an extra finger.

There is controversy today over whether the remains were actually those of Anne Boleyn, but an extra finger was not found with any of the remains exhumed in 1876.

We cannot say that Anne Boleyn definitely did not have six fingers, but it is highly unlikely. In an age of superstition, an extra finger would not have endeared her to the King or his court. It is more likely that she had a small and insignificant blemish on her right hand.

Notes and Sources

- Rise and Growth of the Anglican Schism, Nicholas Sander (1585), p25
- Life of Queen Anne Boleigne, George Wyatt, in George Cavendish's "The Life of Cardinal Wolsey" Volume II (1825), p188
- Notices of the Historic Persons Buried in the Chapel of St Peter ad Vincula in the Tower of London, With an Account of the Discovery of the Supposed Remains of Anne Boleyn, Doyne C. Bell (1877), p19-21, p26

Anne Boleyn and The Other Boleyn Girl

My inspiration for this article comes from a discussion we've been having on The Anne Boleyn Files Facebook page, regarding the inaccuracies of the movie and novel "The Other Boleyn Girl", and from the many emails I receive asking me my thoughts on Philippa Gregory's portrayal of Anne Boleyn.

What concerns me about the emails I receive is that people take "The Other Boleyn Girl" as fact, even though it is marketed as a work of fiction, and I have even heard of people using it for reference when studying Anne Boleyn and the Tudor period!

I realise how tempting it is to take short-cuts when you're studying a topic, e.g. read the study-notes rather than the actual book, but it is extremely dangerous to base your knowledge on something that is a novel and not the true story. I know that Philippa Gregory is seen by many as an historian BUT The Other Boleyn Girl is not a factual retelling of Anne Boleyn's life or even that of Mary Boleyn. Although, in the author's notes at the back of the book Philippa Gregory talks about how her novel is based on theories outlined in Retha Warnicke's book "The Rise and Fall of Anne Boleyn", and various other secondary sources, there are many, many inaccuracies in the book, along with fallacies and story-lines that have no factual basis.

Let's examine some of them...

Mary Boleyn the Virgin

In "The Other Boleyn Girl", Mary Boleyn is the heroine, the "other Boleyn girl" who is telling her story.

The book begins with Mary catching Henry VIII's eye and her family plotting to make Mary his mistress, and the mother of his bastard, to gain status at court. Mary is worried about sleeping with the King as she is so inexperienced. Mary appears innocent and it is Anne who later promises her father and uncle that she will coach her to appeal to the King and satisfy him. "The Other Boleyn Girl" movie opens with Mary just about to marry William Carey and worrying about her wedding night because she is a virgin – not true!

Fact: Most historians believe that Mary had a sexual relationship with King Francis I of France, so she was not a virgin when she arrived back at the English court.

Anne Boleyn Entraps Henry Percy

In the novel, Anne plots to attract Henry Percy so that she can be Duchess of Northumberland and be wealthy. Anne is successful and the couple are betrothed. They then consummate the betrothal to make it legal. Cardinal Wolsey steps in and puts an end to the relationship and Elizabeth Boleyn, Anne's mother, makes Mary forge a letter from Anne to Percy, saying that she has to give him up.

Fact: There is no evidence that Anne set out to trap Percy and it is likely to have been a love match – the two of them meeting at court and falling in love.

Fact: Mary Talbot, Percy's wife, claimed in 1532 that her marriage to Percy was invalid because he was already pre-contracted to marry Anne Boleyn. Henry Percy denied this by swearing an oath on the Blessed Sacrament, in front of the Duke of Norfolk, the archbishops and the King's canon lawyers. There is no evidence that Anne and Henry Percy slept together.

The Boleyn Family Schemers

In "The Other Boleyn Girl" we see Thomas Boleyn, his wife, Elizabeth Boleyn, and her brother, the Duke of Norfolk, having family conferences and scheming, using Mary and Anne as pawns to raise the family's status, what my good friend Rachel Fitzpatrick refers to as "Pimp Daddy Boleyn Syndrome"!

We also see them abandoning Anne to her fate at the end of the novel, with Thomas telling Mary to leave him out of it all because

Anne chose her destiny.

Fact: There is no evidence that the Boleyns/Howards schemed and used the girls as pawns, or that the girls were "coached". It is likely that Mary caught the King's eye with her pretty looks and Anne attracted him with her style and confidence, and that the families made the most of their favour. Women were seen as second-class citizens, and daughters as chattels, but there is nothing to support the view that Thomas Boleyn set out to win favour through Mary and Anne.

Anne Boleyn and Her Sexual Stranglehold Over Henry

In the novel, when Mary is pregnant, Anne is ordered by her family to flirt with the King and keep him happy so that he does not take another mistress, a woman outside of the family. Elizabeth Boleyn tells Mary that Anne has the King wrapped around her little finger. The suggestion is that Anne set out to trap and manipulate Henry VIII on her family's orders and that she held out on him sexually as part of the plan to become queen.

Fact: There is no evidence to support this theory. I personally believe that Henry was attracted to Anne and that she wanted to keep her virtue and not end up like her sister: an abandoned mistress with a bit of a reputation. There is no way that Anne Boleyn could have guessed that Henry would ever offer to make her his wife and queen when she refused to be his mistress - how could she? Henry could have had any woman that he wanted, I'm sure Anne thought he would just move on to the next.

George Boleyn and Incest

The George Boleyn of "The Other Boleyn Girl" has an unnatural relationship with his sisters. He kisses Mary, asking her to kiss him as she does the King, and then he is described as kissing Anne like a lover would. Anne taunts him, suggesting that he wants her sexually. It is all very intimate and inappropriate.

And although we do not have a scene with them actually committing incest, it is clear that we are meant to think that Anne's third pregnancy is a result of incest. Anne tells Mary of how she went to hell and back to conceive and Mary notices a look of guilt pass over George's face. He was obviously part of Anne's plan.

Fact: Anne and George were found guilty of incest at their trial but there is absolutely NO evidence that they committed incest. The majority of historians believe that they were framed and Philippa Gregory is pretty much alone in believing that either of them would have contemplated it. Anne and George were keen reformers and would not have contemplated such an abominable sin.

Anne Boleyn and Incest

In the Q&A section of "The Other Boleyn Girl", Philippa Gregory is asked whether Anne and George really did sleep together so that Anne could conceive. She answers that it is impossible to say but comments that Anne was found guilty of adultery with George and that his own wife, Jane, gave evidence against them. She goes on to say that Anne had already committed murder and she was desperate to provide Henry with a son. Anne needed someone to father that son, so her brother would have been the "obvious choice". What was another sin?

Fact: That answer is wrong in so many ways and on so many levels!!

1. There is no evidence that Jane Boleyn (Jane Parker) gave evidence against George and Anne. It does not appear that any witnesses were called at their trials and Jane is not named as the woman who provided the prosecution with evidence against them, it may well have been the Countess of Worcester.

2. Anne was a very religious person who risked her life and position by having "heretical" books in her possession, there is no way that she would have contemplated the

abominable sin of incest, it would not even have crossed her mind!

3.   What murder?

4.   Why would George be the obvious choice? How many women out there having difficulty conceiving consider sleeping with their brother? Aaaaggghhh!

George Boleyn the Homosexual or Bisexual

It was historian Retha Warnicke who put forward the idea that the men who were executed for adultery with Anne Boleyn were 'libertines' who committed sodomy. In "The Other Boleyn Girl" George not only acts inappropriately with his sisters, he also has a sexual relationship with Sir Francis Weston, a man he's in love with. Later in the novel, Mary knocks on George's locked door and when George opens it, Sir Francis Weston is adjusting his doublet, suggesting that the two men have been enjoying a sexual liaison.

Fact: There is NO evidence that George, or any of the other four men, were homosexual or bisexual. All of the men confessed to being sinners in their execution speeches and Sir Francis Weston mentioned living in "abomination", but I think it is reading too much into their words to accuse them of what were illicit sexual acts.

The Deformed Foetus

In "The Other Boleyn Girl", Anne Boleyn miscarries a deformed baby, a "monster".

Fact: There is no mention of a deformed foetus in the contemporary primary sources. The only historical mention of it is in the writings of Nicholas Sander, a Catholic recusant in Elizabeth I's reign who set out to blacken Anne Boleyn's name. He was also the one who described Anne as having a "projecting tooth", "a large wen" and six fingers. The Imperial ambassador, Eustace Chapuys, who hated Anne and called her "the concubine", simply reported that "the child had the appearance of a male about 3 months and a half old" and Charles Wriothesley said the same. The deformed foetus story is therefore nothing but a myth to make Anne Boleyn appear to be a witch or to back up the story that she had committed adultery or incest.

Anne Boleyn the Bitch

There is no other way to describe the Anne Boleyn of "The Other Boleyn Girl", she is a complete bitch and it's no wonder I get emails asking why I "defend" such a bitch!

Anne steals Henry VIII from Mary and then taunts her. She takes Mary's son away from her without her permission and she treats her siblings like her slaves. She quite likely poisons Bishop Fisher and his dinner guests and perhaps Cardinal Wolsey, Princess Mary and Catherine of Aragon too. She is vindictive when Mary announces her marriage to Will Stafford and her pregnancy, saying that she will tell Mary's son that his mother is dead. And she even curses Jane Seymour, saying that she hopes she dies in childbirth along with her baby. Nice!

Also, in the Q&A section at the back of the book, Philippa Gregory says that Anne would not have let sin get in the way of her plans and that she had committed a murder.

Fact: We do know that Anne had a hot temper and she could be pretty nasty at times, e.g. instructing her aunt to box the ears of the "cursed bastard" (Mary) and starve her if she didn't behave, swearing that she would cure her of her Spanish pride. She even said that she would have Mary put to death while her father was in France, BUT this is a far cry from actually killing someone. Anne was careless with words, she had a quick temper and often said things without thinking. In my opinion, her words were simply bluster, spiteful but no actual truth to them. We've all said things that we regret, and don't really mean, in the heat of the moment! Anne was no angel but she was no murderess either.

Religion

Anne's faith and her reformist views are completely missing from this novel.

Fact: Anne was of reformist views. Her father and brother smuggled heretical books into England from the Continent, her brother translated reformist works for her, Anne helped reformist bishops get positions and she encouraged her ladies to read the Bible, which she left open in her apartments. She may not have been the Protestant martyr or revolutionary that some people think that she was, but there is sufficient evidence to show that she had a real faith.

Anne Boleyn the Witch

In the novel, William Stafford tells Mary that Anne has been involved in witchcraft. We see Anne taking a potion to bring on the miscarriage of her baby which has died in the womb and later in the novel miscarrying a monstrously deformed baby. The midwife who is present when Anne miscarries the "monster" admits to Mary that she has actually been employed by Henry to watch Anne and that she is a "witch taker". However, we never actually see Anne dabbling in witchcraft.

Fact: Giving birth to a deformed baby would have been seen as evidence of sexual sin or witchcraft, but there is no evidence that Anne did give birth to a deformed foetus.

Anne and Henry Carey

In Philippa Gregory's novel, after the death of Mary's husband, William Carey, Anne Boleyn suggests to her sister that she should adopt little Henry Carey. When Mary protests, Anne tells her that it is already done. Mary accuses Anne of stealing the boy so that she has a son to give to the King when they marry.

Fact: Henry VIII appointed Anne Boleyn as Henry Carey's ward in 1528, after the death of his father, William Carey. There was nothing unusual about this. Mary was a widow and Anne was in a position to provide for Henry and she could ensure that her nephew had a good education. He received education at a Cistercian monastery and also under the tutelage of the French poet, Nicholas Bourbon. She did not adopt him. We have discussed it on Facebook and Rachel Fitzpatrick pointed out that it was standard practice for the monarch to grant wardships to wealthy and influential courtiers, e.g. Lady Jane Grey was Thomas Seymour's ward and Catherine Willoughby was Charles Brandon's.

Jane Boleyn

The Jane Boleyn of "The Other Boleyn Girl" is a nasty busybody who is jealous of her husband's relationship with his sisters. In the novel, George is not exactly keen on marrying her and he accuses her of being jealous and being a thief. He also describes how she offered to bring him a girl so that she could watch them have sex and, when he declines, she offers him a boy instead. Apparently, she also likes to eavesdrop. Now, you can see where "The Tudors" got their inspiration for Jane from!

Later in the novel, at Anne Boleyn's fall, Madge Shelton tells Mary Boleyn of how Jane was interrogated the longest and that she wrote and signed a statement. Madge goes on to say that after Jane was questioned the other maids were called in again and asked about George. The reader is then told of Jane providing the evidence that was used to convict George, the evidence which led to his death

Fact: There is no evidence to support this characterization of Jane Boleyn and Jane did not confess to lying about George and Anne in her execution speech, that is a myth. Jane did tell Cromwell of Anne's indiscretion about Henry's sexual inadequacies, but we don't know what else Jane told Cromwell and it is time to stop using her as a scapegoat.

Lack of Maternal Love

In "The Other Boleyn Girl", Anne Boleyn is horrified when she gives birth to a daughter,. A girl is useless. There is also no relationship between Anne and Elizabeth in the novel. Anne seems to lack maternal love and there is an awful scene where Anne strips little Elizabeth half naked to prove to everyone that she is perfect and beautiful, Elizabeth's lip is trembling as Anne rages at Henry.

Fact: It was Henry VIII who paraded his naked baby daughter in front of ambassadors to show how perfect she was. Also, Anne loved her daughter dearly and was a keen and good mother in the short time she had with her. Historians David Starkey and Tracy Borman refer to a story of how Anne Boleyn wanted to defy convention by breastfeeding her baby herself, but was prevented from doing so by her husband. Tracy Borman also writes of how courtiers were often embarrassed by Anne's displays of affection for her baby and that she loved to have Elizabeth next to her on a cushion, rather than shut away, out of sight and mind, in a nursery, and when Elizabeth was given her own household at Hatfield, Anne spent time carefully choosing fabrics for her daughter's clothes and visited her whenever possible.

The Movie

"The Other Boleyn Girl" movie, starring Eric Bana, Natalie Portman and Scarlett Johansson is even worse for historical inaccuracies:-

- Henry VIII rapes Anne Boleyn
- Anne making Henry promise that he'd never speak to Mary again after she's given birth to his son
- Mary Boleyn intercedes on Anne's behalf and tries to get her pardon
- Mary Boleyn walks into court and takes Elizabeth at the end

It makes me cringe and shout at the TV!

Don't Knock Historical Fiction!

I know I'm going to get people saying that there's nothing wrong with historical fiction and that I shouldn't criticise it because people should be able to distinguish fact from fiction and I'm really not having a go at historical fiction. My bookcase is full of historical fiction: Jean Plaidy, C J Sansom, Robin Maxwell, Jeane Westin etc. BUT those authors are not saying that their novels are true and they carefully explain where they have deviated from the truth in their notes. Reading Philippa Gregory's notes and interviews, she is suggesting that she is an historian and that "The Other Boleyn Girl" is not a distortion of the facts, but is a retelling of Anne and Mary's story, and that is why I have such a big problem with this particular novel.

So, if you know someone who thinks they know Anne Boleyn's story from reading "The Other Boleyn Girl" or you know a student who is doing a project on Anne Boleyn, point them to a website like The Anne Boleyn Files. I am committed to telling Anne Boleyn's true story by researching primary sources and the works of Tudor historians like Eric Ives, David Starkey and David Loades.

Notes and Sources

- The Other Boleyn Girl by Philippa Gregory
- Elizabeth, David Starkey
- Elizabeth's Women: The Hidden Story of the Virgin Queen, Tracy Borman

"The Tudors" – Is it Really So Bad?

It's interesting the reaction you get from people when you mention the hit TV series "The Tudors". In fact, in my experience there are three main reactions:-

- A lighting up of the eyes and excitement – These are the people who rave about how wonderful Jonathan Rhys Meyers is, what a great Anne Boleyn Natalie Dormer was, how sexy Henry Cavill is... etc. etc. and how wonderful the programme is at portraying the Tudor period warts and all.

- Shock and horror – People who believe that "The Tudors" is pretty much a swear word – David Starkey publicly lambasted the series for its inaccuracies and he's not the only one who felt strongly about it. In many circles, if you mention that you watch "The Tudors" then that's pretty much saying that you are not serious about history and you may even get thrown off forums and discussion boards.

- A balanced appreciation – There are those (like me!) who love "The Tudors" for what it is – entertainment! I love its richness and vibrancy, the way it brings the characters to life, the way it portrays life at the Tudor Court and the way it makes it so real. Yes, it is littered with inaccuracies, but as Anne Boleyn Files visitor Gemma pointed out, it also has many accuracies. Gemma pointed out about the episode where Henry falls in the river and gets his head stuck in the mud – an event that really happened but that not many people knew about previously.

The reason I'm writing about "The Tudors" today is because Tudor historian Dr Tracy Borman has written an article for "The Radio Times" (copied in the BBC History Magazine) defending the series. Wow, an historian saying she likes it!!

In her article, "The Truth Behind "The Tudors"", Borman writes of how she was determined to hate it but found herself coming to appreciate it as "an historical drama". She commented on the liberties it took with the historical facts but applauded the way that it brought Henry VIII and his court to life.

Borman also makes the point that I have often made about how the series has had a positive effect in that it is stimulating people's interest in the Tudor period. She writes of how Hampton Court Palace has seen a surge in visitor numbers and how the show even has its own wiki site. People are crying out for information on the era and the characters and, as owner of a Tudor history website, I can testify to this! I even have a friend who rings me after she's watched "The Tudors" (she calls me her Historical Oracle!) to ask if events really did happen.

Borman goes on to say that TV series, movies and fiction can bring people into history and encourage people to find out the truth behind the story. That they can be useful. I wholeheartedly agree with her. I'm sure that if we looked at the sales figures for Tudor history books and the number of Google searches done on "Tudor", "Henry VIII" etc., we would see a significant rise as people want to know what really happened. Also, is it any coincidence that so many Tudor history books are being published at the moment?

Another criticism of "The Tudors" is that it's a bit like a soap opera, but then what else would you call Henry VIII's life? I'm showing my age now, but Henry is a lot more interesting than JR Ewing!

I can't criticise "The Tudors", I think I would be two-faced if I did, because there are some of you out there who have set out on your mission to find out about Anne Boleyn because "The Tudors" piqued your interest and you found this site! If "The Tudors" helps to get people interested in Anne, if it helps me to spread the message about her and share the truth then long live "The Tudors"!

Notes and Sources

- The Truth Behind "The Tudors", HistoryExtra.com
- The Tudors, Showtime, written by Michael Hirst

The Six Wives' Stereotypes

It's not just Anne Boleyn who has been misrepresented by history, TV, film and fiction, I think every single one of the six wives has been misrepresented. Here are some of the labels, stereotypes and myths which the general public believe regarding these 16th century women:-

- Catherine of Aragon – The wronged woman, the pious queen, the stubborn ex-wife who caused her daughter's ill-treatment and who was to blame for Mary's shortcomings and brutal reign, the boring one.

- Anne Boleyn – The whore, the witch, the murderess, the adulteress, the one who slept with her brother out of desperation, the one with six fingers, the bitch, the other woman, the home-wrecker... or, alternatively, the martyr, the saint, the heroine and the one responsible for the English Reformation.

- Jane Seymour – The meek, mild, virtuous, conservative queen who was as boring as she was plain, the only one who gave Henry a son.

- Anne of Cleves – The Flanders Mare who was so ugly that Henry VIII couldn't even bring himself to sleep with her!

- Catherine Howard – The tart, the airhead, the nymphomaniac, the stupid one who deserved all she got.

- Catherine Parr – The mature nursemaid who nursed Henry in his last years, the one who got away.

See what I mean? None of those labels are correct, are they? And don't these women deserve for these myths to be debunked and for people to hear their real stories? I think so.

Catherine of Aragon – The Boring One?

I thought that I would write about the six wives and the various stereotypes, labels, myths and falsehoods which surround them. I will handle each wife in turn, in the order that Henry VIII married them. I'll start by looking at Catherine of Aragon.

Labels, Stereotypes and Representations

If you stood in a shopping centre and asked passers-by for their opinion on Catherine of Aragon, I'm not quite sure what reaction you'd get; possibly a lot of 'Who?'s. It may be that popular fiction and programmes like "The Tudors" have somewhat enlightened people about the first of Henry's wives:- but have they been truly enlightened, or have they ended up with a rather warped picture of her? It's hard to say. Some of the stereotyping, labels, opinions and myths I come across include:-

- Catherine was overly pious and religious
- Catherine was stubborn and was responsible for the break with Rome and the cruelty of her daughter's reign
- She was boring
- Catherine had loads of miscarriages and/or she was barren
- She was much older than Henry
- Her marriage to Henry was short-lived
- Catherine was poisoned by Anne Boleyn
- Catherine was a liar, claiming she had not consummated her marriage to Arthur
- She was dowdy
- She had dark hair and dark eyes, the typical Spanish looks
- Her marriage to Henry was loveless

So, let's look at some of these issues and try to unravel who Catherine of Aragon really was...

Catherine of Aragon's Appearance

Although Catherine was the daughter of the Catholic Reyes of Spain, early portraits depict her with long, auburn or strawberry blonde hair*, fair skin and blue eyes, rather than the typical dark looks and olive skins of Spaniards. These looks were inherited from her English Royal ancestors, women like her great-grandmother and name-sake, Catherine of Lancaster, and her great-great-grandmother, Philippa of Lancaster. Her figure may have become 'stouter' in later years, after her pregnancies, but whose body doesn't change after at least six pregnancies? She certainly was not dowdy when Henry married her in 1509.

Catherine's Faith

As, David Starkey points out, Catherine was very much her mother's daughter as far as her faith was concerned. She had seen her parents expel the Jews from Granada in 1492 and had seen them fight the Moors. She was a staunch Catholic.[1] She believed in fighting heresy, whatever that involved, but there was nothing unusual in that. David Starkey writes of how she believed that faith was God's gift and that the Church needed to defend and protect God's Truth.[2]

Catherine's Church was committed to fighting heresy and Catherine, like Thomas More, believed that heresy needed to be dealt with severely, even if that meant that the punishment was death.[3] In our age of tolerance and our multicultural and multifaith world, we perceive Catherine and Thomas More as intolerant, bigots even. However they were simply products of their time, people of faith who were doing what the Church taught, God's work.

Catherine's faith consoled and sustained her when her husband had his extramarital affairs and when he abandoned her for Anne Boleyn. We cannot criticise her for turning to God at such a time. At least her relationship with God gave her some comfort in those dark days, particularly the time when she was not even allowed to see her daughter.

Catherine's Virginity

As David Starkey points out in his book on Henry's six wives, only God knows what happened between Catherine and Arthur on their wedding night. Sir Anthony Willoughby, a servant of Arthur's, claimed that on the morning after the wedding night, Arthur had bragged about sleeping with Catherine,[4] but was he simply boasting to keep up appearances? Was it just bravado? We don't know for sure. What *is* certain is that it was taken for granted at the time that Catherine and Arthur had done the deed. However, Doña Elvira, Catherine's First Lady of the Bedchamber, wrote to Catherine's parents after Arthur's death, telling them that their daughter was still a virgin.

The consummation or non-consummation of Catherine's first marriage was not an issue when she married Henry VIII in 1509 because the couple were given a dispensation by the Pope. However, the topic reared its ugly head when Henry VIII wanted to annul his marriage to Catherine so that he could marry his new love, Anne Boleyn. Henry argued that the dispensation should never have been given and was invalid because marrying one's brother's widow was contrary to Biblical law. Catherine, on the other hand, argued that she had never slept with Arthur and so the marriage had never been fully legal. While the Blackfriars legatine court heard how Catherine must have consummated her marriage to Arthur, another court in Zaragoza, Spain, in 1531, heard from witnesses who had travelled to England with Catherine on her initial voyage, and who argued that Arthur was a sickly young man who couldn't cope with the expectations people had of his wedding night.[5] It was all too much for him. As Giles Tremlett points out, the witnesses could have been lying, but then so could have the witnesses at Blackfriars.

Catherine testified on oath that she had not slept with her first husband, saying that when she married Henry, she had been a virgin. She had also told Henry VII that she was still a maid when he was first thinking of marrying her off to his second son. In her book on

Henry's six wives, Alison Weir argues that Catherine's principles and religious beliefs would not have allowed her to lie and that she was probably speaking the truth.[6] I have to agree with her.

Catherine's Age

Catherine of Aragon was born on the 16th December 1485 making her only five and a half years older than her second husband, Henry VIII. She was just 23 when they married in 1509, but obviously, in 1528 when Henry began his quest of an annulment in earnest, Catherine was 43, compared to her husband's age of 37. Catherine was old for Tudor times and had also gone through the menopause. Henry, on the other hand, felt that he was still in his prime, and was in love with Anne Boleyn, a woman in her 20s and, more importantly, a woman who was still capable of child-bearing. So, although Catherine was not much older than her husband, she had lost her beauty, her allure and her fertility.

Trivia: When Season 1 of "The Tudors" premiered on TV, Maria Doyle Kennedy, who plays Catherine of Aragon, was 43 and Jonathan Rhys Meyers, who played her husband, Henry VIII, was just 30, a 13 year difference!

A Love Match

Although their betrothal had originally been arranged by Henry VII and Catherine's parents, it was Henry VIII who decided to marry Catherine after his accession to the throne in 1509. It was his choice and I think he saw himself as the chivalrous hero rescuing the damsel in distress, a woman who was living in debt and uncertainty. Alison Weir writes of how Henry, when discussing the marriage with his Privy Council, told of how he loved Catherine and how he wanted to marry her.[7] His council knew that he had been smitten with her since the age of ten. Weir concludes that he obviously found her attractive and that he realised that her lineage and character made her a suitable consort.

Programmes like "The Tudors" do not give us a full picture of

Catherine and Henry's marriage. It was happy in the beginning and they had been married for 24 years when their marriage was finally annulled in 1533. Although Henry was unfaithful to Catherine, for example with women like Bessie Blount and Mary Boleyn, he loved and respected his wife. Having mistresses was his royal prerogative and was a way of fulfilling his sexual urges when his wife was pregnant or recovering from childbirth.

Catherine loved Henry and thought of him as her true husband and her true love right to the end. Her last letter** to him, written when she was dying, speaks of her tender love for him, the fact that she forgives him and ends with her saying that the thing she wanted most was to see him again. No matter how cruelly he treated her, Catherine loved him with all her heart.

Catherine's Pregnancies

Henry VIII believed (or had convinced himself!) that his marriage to Catherine was cursed and that God was not blessing them with a surviving male heir because their marriage was contrary to Biblical law. So, what was Catherine's obstetric history?

Historian J.J. Scarisbrick[8] wrote of how Catherine of Aragon had experienced several miscarriages and had lost three babies through stillbirths and two in early infancy. She had had one successful pregnancy: Princess Mary. Hester Chapman[9] wrote of Catherine having a total of seven pregnancies, Neville Williams[10] wrote of Henry VIII worrying about earlier miscarriages in his second year of marriage to Catherine, A.F.Pollard[11] suggests around ten pregnancies and John Bowle[12] states six pregnancies. However, in his article "The Alleged Miscarriages of Catherine of Aragon and Anne Boleyn",[13] Professor Sir John Dewhurst argues that there is only evidence for six pregnancies:-

1. 31st January 1510 – Birth of a stillborn daughter. This is reported by Diego Fernandez, Catherine's chancellor, in the Calendar of State Papers (Spain)

2. 1st January 1511 – Birth of a son, Henry, Duke of Cornwall,

who died on 22nd February at just 52 days old.

3.   17th September 1513 – Birth of a son who was either stillborn or who died shortly after birth. The Venetian Calendar of State Papers records that the child was alive at birth: "a male heir was born to the King of England and will inherit the crown, the other son having died."

4.   November 1514 – The Venetian Ambassador reported that "The Queen has been delivered of a stillborn male child of eight months to the very great grief of the whole court", the chronicler, Holinshed, wrote that "in November the Queen was delivered of a prince which lived not long after", and John Stow wrote "in the meantime, to Whit, the month of November, the Q was delivered of a prince which lived not long after".

5.   18th February - Birth of Princess Mary.

6.   10th November 1518 – The stillbirth of a daughter. The Venetian ambassador wrote "The Queen has been delivered in her eighth month of a stillborn daughter to the great sorrow of the nation at large".

OK, so she hadn't had much success but it's not a huge list of miscarriages and it shows that she did not have fertility problems until after 1518 when she was in her 30s, when it seems that she entered the menopause.

Contrary to popular belief, Catherine did provide her husband with a living son: Henry, Duke of Cornwall. He only lived for 52 days, but was healthy at birth and was christened. Perhaps he was a victim of cot death (SIDS), we do not know.

Boring?

Catherine is often portrayed as a woman with fading looks whose only interest was praying. However she was an intelligent woman who had received an excellent education and she enjoyed hunting (particularly with a hawk), music (listening to it rather than playing), dancing and playing cards, dice, backgammon and other such pastimes. She also took an active part in the masques and entertainments planned by her husband. In his chapter "Party Queen", Giles Tremlett writes of how Henry surprised his wife in 1524 by dressing up as Robin Hood, dressing his men as outlaws, and bursting in on his wife and her ladies in Catherine's chambers. A surprised Catherine humoured her husband and threw an impromptu party.

Although she was not a fashion trendsetter, like Anne Boleyn, it is clear that she loved jewels and fine clothes. She was also popular with both her staff and the English people.

Catherine of Aragon was also an active queen, not just an accessory on her husband's arm. In 1513, when Henry VIII went to fight in France, he left his wife as Regent and she did not fail him. On the 22nd August, James IV, taking advantage of Henry's absence, took 80,000 soldiers with him over the border from Scotland to England. An English force, led by the Earl of Surrey, travelled north and on the 9th September defeated the Scots at the Battle of Flodden and killed the King of the Scots. Catherine sent James IV's bloody coat and banner to her husband in France – she had been victorious and had successfully defended England in the absence of her husband.

Catherine was also active in the organising and overseeing of her daughter Mary's education. In her biography of Mary, Linda Porter[9] writes of how Catherine had "considerable input into her curriculum" and that she commissioned the Spanish humanist, Juan Luis Vives to write a book on female education, "The Education of a Christian Woman".

Catherine of Aragon Scandals and Interesting tidbits

You may associate scandals with wives like Anne Boleyn and Catherine Howard, but Catherine's life too was, and is, surrounded by scandal and gossip, for example:-

- Did she have an eating disorder? – In his biography of Catherine and his article for The Daily Mail, "Was Henry VIII's first wife anorexic? Catherine of Aragon's secret problem",[14] Giles Tremlett theorises that Catherine's eating problems could have led to fertility problems which prevented her from producing the much needed male heir.

- Was she rather too close to her confessor? – In the period between Arthur's death and her marriage to Henry VIII, Catherine was very dependent on and close to her confessor, the young Spanish friar, Fray Diego Fernández. Giles Tremlett writes of how Catherine became "infatuated" with her confessor and let him control her, although she would never have had an affair [15] with him. Gossip surrounded their close relationship, due to the fact that Diego had a reputation as a bit of a womaniser. However, Diego became forgotten when Catherine married Henry VIII, a man she obviously loved and was besotted with.

- Did she sleep with Arthur? – Did she or didn't she? Did she lie or was she a maid when she married Henry VIII? This question is still being debated today.

Catherine's Death – Murder by Poison?

Eustace Chapuys, the Imperial Ambassador and friend to Catherine of Aragon, had reported to the Emperor in January 1536 that he "feared the concubine, who had often sworn to take away their lives, and who will never rest until she has accomplished her object, believing, as she did, and does still, that, owing to this King's capricious humour and temper, her position will not be secure as long as the two ladies, mother and daughter, live. She would then have better opportunities than before of executing her damnable purpose, by having poison of some sort administered to them"[16]

When Catherine died in January 1536, the chandler who examined her body found her heart to be black with a strange growth attached to it. Although most historians today believe that

Catherine died of cancer, it was believed that the black heart was evidence that the former queen had been poisoned. Since she had felt sick after a glass of Welsh ale, the gossip was that the ale was to blame and that Anne Boleyn had a hand in it.

A Queen to be Admired

Alison Weir writes of how Catherine's strong character, her devotion and courage, are admired today even though we may see them as "misplaced".[17]

To our modern eyes, Catherine appears a religious fanatic, a victim, a woman who wallowed in her misery and would not let go of her marriage. Many blame her for the woman her daughter Mary became, an intolerant and cruel queen. People say that she should have accepted the failure of her marriage and gone into a convent, and that doing so would have saved her and her daughter a lot of grief, but, we have the benefit of hindsight; we know how the story ended and what a damaged woman Mary became.

We are also looking on the situation with our 21st century eyes and not taking into account the times Catherine lived in or the beliefs that surrounded marriage. As I have said before, Catherine and Henry had made their vows before God and so there marriage was a binding contract for life, something that could not and should not be broken. Catherine would not risk her soul by accepting the annulment and prayed that Henry would come to his senses so that his soul could also be saved. Catherine also believed that her daughter was the rightful heir to the throne and so fought for her claim. Accepting the annulment would have meant accepting her daughter's illegitimacy and her removal from the succession, and Catherine just could not do that.

Catherine stood up to her bully of a husband even when he took her title from her, took her jewellery from her to give to his new love, separated her from her daughter, sent her to a cold, dark castle, reduced her staff, ignored her and tried to bully her and Mary into submission. For that, she should be admired. She stuck to her principles and her beliefs against a man who went on to execute two wives. She was prepared to die a martyr if she had to and I admire her strength and her courage.

So, Catherine the boring wife? I don't think so!

If you want to know more about Catherine of Aragon I highly recommend Giles Tremlett's biography on her. Catherine was popular and loved by her people and she deserves to be today. I hate seeing "Team Catherine" versus "Team Anne" type arguments online, e.g. arguing over how much air-time the ghosts of the two queens had in the final episode of "The Tudors", how ridiculous! We can be fascinated and obsessed with Anne Boleyn, but still admire Henry's other wives and remember them in a right and fitting manner.

Notes and Sources

*The recording herald at her entry into London prior to her marriage to Arthur described her long, auburn hair.[18]

**Giles Tremlett doubts the authenticity of this letter, but, in my opinion, it does sound like Catherine and I hope she wrote it.

1. Six Wives: The Queens of Henry VIII, David Starkey
2. Ibid.
3. Ibid.
4. Ibid.
5. Catherine of Aragon: Henry's Spanish Queen, Giles Tremlett
6. The Six Wives of Henry VIII, Alison Weir
7. Ibid
8. Henry VIII, J.J. Scarisbrick
9. Anne Boleyn, Hester Chapman
10. Henry VIII and His Court, Neville Williams
11. John Bowle in The Alleged Miscarriages of Catherine of Aragon and Anne Boleyn, Sir John Dewhurst, Medical

History, 1984

12. The Alleged Miscarriages of Catherine of Aragon and Anne Boleyn, Sir John Dewhurst, Medical History, 1984

13. The Myth of "Bloody Mary": A Biography of Queen Mary I of England, Linda Porter, Chapter 2 "The Education of a Princess"

14. "Was Henry VlllU+2019s first wife anorexic? Catherine of Aragon's secret problem", Giles Tremlett, Mail Online, 6th November 2010

15. Tremlett

16. Calendar of State Papers, Spain, Volume 5 Part 2: 1536-1538, 9

17. Weir

18. Starkey

Anne Boleyn –
The Mysterious and Maligned One

There's no denying that Anne Boleyn is the most maligned and misunderstood of Henry VIII's six wives. Even today, in an age where we have unprecedented access to primary sources and the likes of historians Eric Ives and Alison Weir are spreading the message that Anne Boleyn was innocent and framed, Anne Boleyn is still misrepresented in fiction, non-fiction, TV programmes, movies, radio shows, podcasts and online. I am regularly asked why I feel the need to dedicate my time to researching and writing about an historical character who was a traitor to the crown and a home-wrecker.

So, what are the labels that Anne Boleyn is wrongly given?

- Whore – The imperial ambassador never referred to Anne Boleyn by name and instead called her "the concubine", "the she-devil" and "the whore", the Abbot of Whitby called her "Common stewed [professional] whore", a lady called Margaret Chanseler referred to Anne as "The Goggle Eyed Whore" and she was also known as "The Great Whore", "The King's Whore" and a "naughty paike"!

- "The Scandal of Christendom" – This is what Catherine of Aragon called Anne.

- Home-wrecker or 'the other woman' – This is the kind of label you see in Team Catherine versus Team Anne type arguments. People who give Anne this label feel that Anne purposely broke up Henry's marriage to Catherine.

- Seductress, plotter, tease and sexual predator – The belief that Anne Boleyn set out to purposely seduce and trap Henry VIII so that she could be queen.

- Poisoner – In "The Other Boleyn Girl", Philippa Gregory, suggests that Anne poisoned Bishop Fisher and his dinner guests, Cardinal Wolsey and Catherine of Aragon.

- Witch – The idea that Anne Boleyn was a witch who put Henry under a spell. If you are eagle-eyed, you will have spotted Anne Boleyn's portrait on the wall of Hogwarts in the first Harry Potter film, "Harry Potter and the Philosopher's Stone" (The Sorcerer's Stone).

- Deformed – Nicholas Sander, a Catholic recusant in Elizabeth I's reign, wrote of Anne Boleyn having six fingers, a projecting tooth and a large wen under her chin.

- Adulteress – Anne was charged with adultery and incest and some people believe that 'there's no smoke without a fire'.

- Traitor – She was executed as a traitor, as someone who had not only committed adultery and slept with her brother, but also as someone who had plotted against the king.

- Bigamist – In "The Other Boleyn Girl", Anne Boleyn marries Henry Percy and they consummate their union, therefore, according to Philippa Gregory, Anne was a bigamist.

- Kidnapper – In "The Other Boleyn Girl" (do you get the idea that many of the stereotypes and labels can be blamed on this novel?!), Anne adopts her sister Mary's son, Henry, without Mary's permission. She steals him.

- That she gave birth to a monster – The idea that Anne gave birth to a monstrously deformed baby and that this was a sign that she had committed incest or was a witch.

And I'm sure you can think of more. But those who seek to avenge Anne Boleyn also make her out to be someone she is not:-

- Protestant martyr and saint – One website (Reformation. org) claims that Anne's "only 'crime' was breaking up an incestuous relationship between King Henry VIII and Catherine of Aragon", that her death was part of a conspiracy to keep England under the Catholic Church, that her doctor made sure that she did not have a male heir and that Anne should therefore be seen as a saint and martyr.

- Victim of poison – The same website I mentioned a minute ago speaks of how Anne was given the cantarella of Borgia (poison) to make her miscarry.

- A Sibyl or prophetess – I heard that one radio show on Anne Boleyn was claiming that Margaret of Austria ran a spiritual academy for sibyls (seeresses and prophetesses), a Renaissance version of Hogwarts, and that Anne was educated as a sibyl and groomed to be queen.

- The Leader of the Reformation in England – Some people believe that not only was Anne groomed to be queen by the likes of Margaret of Austria and Marguerite of Angoulême, but that she was also groomed to break the Catholic Church in England and lead the Reformation.

- Vampire – I had to add this as there seems to be a trend at the moment in fiction for Tudor characters to be portrayed as vampires. A kind of Twilight meets Sookie Stackhouse meets The Other Boleyn Girl! Hmm...

Reading through that list, I'm not sure which is worse: the labels given to her by those who sought (or seek) to discredit her or the ones used by Anne Boleyn "avengers"!

Obviously, at the end of the day, we are never going to know who the real Anne Boleyn was because we just don't have the primary sources to give us that full picture. Our theories, and those of historians and academics, are just that, theories, based on our interpretation of the sources. If you look at how two esteemed historians like Eric Ives and G W Bernard can disagree over Anne, then you can see what a minefield the subject of Anne Boleyn is. Anyway, I digress, let's look at these labels and the truth behind them...

Anne Boleyn the Whore

It's easy to understand why Eustace Chapuys would label Anne "the whore" or "the concubine" because his allegiance was with Charles V, Catherine of Aragon's nephew, and therefore with Catherine and Mary. In his opinion, Anne was the evil other woman, the woman who had led Henry VIII astray, and he did not recognise their marriage. Also, think about the general public, the people who had had Catherine as their queen for over 20 years. She was well respected and popular and Anne, in their opinion, had usurped her position. Just think about the public's reaction to Camilla Parker-Bowles when they found out that Prince Charles had always loved her and had spent his honeymoon with Diana ringing Camilla. Also consider that the royal family are concerned that Camilla will never be recognised as queen by the British public. Yet we are in the 21st century, a time where divorce is a fact of life. I know it's not quite the same, but it does help us to understand people's reaction to Anne Boleyn and the fact that she was labelled a whore, even though it is pretty clear that she was a virtuous woman who tried to refuse the King's advances.

The Scandal of Christendom

Catherine called Anne Boleyn "The Scandal of Chrisendom". It was an understandable reaction from Catherine. She's not exactly going to praise the woman who has caught her husband's eye and who is the cause of all her woes. Just look at what happened to Catherine and her daughter, it's easy to see why they held Anne accountable for the annulment, their loss of status and the cruel treatment they suffered. Once Anne was dead and gone, Mary had a rude awakening when she realised that it was her father who was ultimately responsible for her treatment, when things got worse instead of better. It is understandable that Catherine blamed Anne because she loved her husband and Mary loved her father, but it doesn't make their assessment of Anne a true one. Now, I'm not trying to paint Anne as an angel, as she certainly was not. She said spiteful things and she flew into rages, making rash threats against Catherine and Mary. We have to hold Henry accountable for what happened to these women really.

Home-wrecker

The people who label Anne as a "home-wrecker" are people who look at the love triangle with 21st century eyes. What we have to remember is:-

- There were rumours of Henry VIII annulling his marriage to Catherine in 1514, long before Anne came on the scene and he had already stopped sleeping with his wife.

- Anne did not chase Henry, she did not initiate the affair and she actually said "no" to begin with.

- Henry had already concluded that his marriage was not valid or legal, that it was incestuous,

- Anne had no choice – She tried saying no and it didn't work, she tried retreating to Hever and that didn't work, Henry always got what he wanted and he was the King.

So, please let's blame Henry for the deterioration and subsequent end of his marriage, not Anne Boleyn.

Sexual Predator

I think this idea stems from books and films like "The Other Boleyn Girl", where we see Anne purposely throwing herself at Henry VIII while Mary is pregnant so that the Boleyns still have influence. In the book, Elizabeth Boleyn describes Anne as controlling Henry, of playing with him. We come away with the idea that Henry is powerless and that Anne's sexuality gives her all the power, that she is calling the shots. Well, anyone who knows anything about a woman's place in Tudor England and about Henry VIII knows that although Anne may have been an influence on Henry she certainly was not the one pulling the strings.

Author Karen Lindsey ("Divorced, Beheaded, Survived: A Feminist Reinterpretation of the Wives of Henry VIII") goes as far as saying that Anne Boleyn could have been the victim of sexual harassment. Henry was infatuated with Anne, he wrote her 17 letters, when he usually hated writing, and he complains in those letters about Anne not replying to him and rejecting his advances. Lindsey writes that Anne had no choice in what happened to her, Henry was the one in power and Anne would have been risking her father's and brother's court careers if she had refused his advances. She had to give in.

Lindsey goes on to explain that Anne really was a creature being hunted by the King and there was no escape for her. I agree to a point, Anne was definitely more prey than predator. Henry fell for her and he wanted her. He was not used to someone saying no to him and did not give up. He pursued her relentlessly. Of course, we don't know what Anne's feelings were, as we only have his letters, but it is clear from those that he had to persuade her into the relationship. However, I don't see Anne as a victim of sexual harassment, just the object of a very passionate man's affections, and I think she was flattered by him and then fell in love with him. They shared many interests and they were very alike at that time, so it was a very natural partnership.

Poisoner and Murderess

In "The Other Boleyn Girl" book, Mary Boleyn is told by her husband, that Anne poisoned Bishop Fisher and his household, and that she was responsible for the deaths of three men. He also accuses Anne of poisoning Cardinal Wolsey and Catherine of Aragon.

In her notes on the book, Philippa Gregory writes of how Anne Boleyn was guilty of at least one murder – who? There is absolutely no evidence that Anne tried to poison anyone and she was not charged with murder or attempted murder at her trial. There were rumours that Catherine of Aragon had died of poisoning after it was found that her heart was black and that her illness had worsened after drinking some Welsh ale. After Anne's fall, Henry VIII led Henry Fitzroy to believe that Anne had planned to poison him and his half-sister, Mary, but there was no basis to these accusations. Catherine died of cancer and Henry VIII was just ranting and blustering – he also spoke of Anne having 100 lovers!

A Witch with Six Fingers

OK, just because Anne Boleyn's portrait is on the wall at Hogwarts it does not mean that she was really a witch – ha! Seriously, although Henry VIII said to a courtier that he had been "seduced and constrained by sortilèges", sortilèges meaning "sorcery, spells or charms", and that his marriage must be cursed because he had not been blessed with a son, it does not mean that he believed that Anne was a witch. In her book "1536: The Year that Changed Henry VIII", Suzannah Lipscomb writes of how, at the time, "sortilèges" meant "divination" and that Henry could have meant that prophecies regarding Anne bearing sons had led him to marry her. Of course, Henry could simply have been referring to his infatuation with Anne, how she had bewitched him and entranced him.

In "The Rise and Fall of Anne Boleyn", Retha Warnicke writes of how Anne Boleyn gave birth to a deformed foetus in 1536, what Nicholas Sander describes as a "shapeless mass of flesh", and that this was a sign that Anne used witchcraft and that she had committed some kind of sexual sin. When we combine that with the fact that Sander describes Anne as having six fingers, a projecting tooth and a wen under her chin, then it makes us wonder where she hid the black cat and broomstick!

There is a "but" of course, and it's a big but – BUT, there is NO evidence that Anne miscarried a deformed foetus or that she had six fingers etc etc! Nicholas Sander did not even know Anne (he was born around 1530) and he was a Catholic recusant writing during the reign of Anne's daughter, Elizabeth I. His aim was to discredit Elizabeth by blackening her mother's name. Surely, the rather paranoid and vain Henry VIII would not have considered marrying a disfigured woman, never mind breaking with Rome for her, and you would think that Chapuys would have joyously spread the news of Anne's monstrous baby, rather than describing it as a male child of around 3 and a half months in gestation. Need I say more?

Adulteress and Traitor

At her trial, on the 15th May 1536, Anne Boleyn was accused of incest, adultery, promising to marry Norris after the King's death, plotting the King's death and laughing at the King and his dress. Although Anne protested her innocence, a jury of her peers (or rather her enemies!) found her guilty and she was sentenced to death. The men that she was said to have committed adultery with had already been found guilty, so her trial was completely prejudiced, and the executioner had been ordered from Calais before her trial had even taken place.

If you consider that the dates of Anne's offences listed in the indictment make no sense, that even the man who called her "the concubine" did not believe she was guilty, that Henry was off gallivanting with ladies (and Jane Seymour) and that Anne's household was broken up before the trial, then her guilt was definitely a foregone conclusion. The majority of historians believe that Anne was innocent and that she was framed, I agree wholeheartedly.

Bigamist

No! Anne may have been in love with Henry Percy and the couple may well have been planning to marry BUT Cardinal Wolsey and Percy's father, the Earl of Northumberland, put a stop to the relationship and Percy was married off to Mary Talbot. According to a letter written by Chapuys in July 1532, Henry Percy had to deny, in front of the whole council, that there had been a pre-contract between himself and Anne Boleyn, after his wife reported that he had claimed, during a quarrel, that their marriage was not real because he had been legally contracted to Anne Boleyn. Percy also denied the pre-contract in 1536 when Archbishop Cranmer questioned him. There is, therefore, no evidence that Anne and Percy had been pre-contracted or that they had consummated their union (à la "The Other Boleyn Girl").

Kidnapper

Another "The Other Boleyn Girl" misrepresentation of Anne. is that she was a kidnapper. In the book, after the death of Mary Boleyn's first husband, Anne Boleyn adopts Mary's son, Henry Carey, without Mary's permission. She steals him. The truth behind this accusation is that Henry VIII appointed Anne Boleyn as Henry Carey's guardian in 1528, after the death of his father, William Carey. This was nothing unusual. Mary Boleyn was a widow and Anne was in a position to provide for Mary's son and to ensure that he had a good education. As Anne Boleyn Files visitor Rachel Fitzpatrick pointed out, it was standard practice for the King to grant wardships to wealthy and influential courtiers, for example, Lady Jane Grey was Thomas Seymour's ward and Catherine Willoughby was Charles Brandon's.

Protestant Martyr and Saint

As I said earlier, Reformation.org call Anne Saint Anne Boleyn and write of how her story mirrors that of the Biblical Queen Esther in that anne risked her life to bring the Gospel to Henry.

The martryologist, John Foxe, wrote of Anne Boleyn in his Book of Martyrs (Actes and Monuments):-

"Godly I call her, for sundry respects, whatsoever the cause was, or quarrel objected against her. First, her last words spoken at her death declared no less her sincere faith and trust in Christ, than did her quiet modesty utter forth the goodness of the cause and matter, whatsoever it was. Besides that to such as wisely can judge upon cases occurrent, this also may seem to give a great clearing unto her, that the king, the third day after, was married in his whites unto another. Certain this was, that for the rare and singular gifts of her mind, so well instructed, and given toward God, with such a fervent desire unto the truth and setting forth of sincere religion, joined with like gentleness, modesty, and pity toward all men, there have not many such queens before her borne the crown of England. Principally this one commendation she left behind her, that during her life, the religion of Christ most happily flourished, and had a right prosperous course."

But however much we admire Anne, and however much she helped to promote reformist ideas and encourage the reading of the English Bible, she did not die because of her faith. Dictionary. com defines "martyr" (in the sense we mean) as:-

- A person who willingly suffers death rather than renounce his or her religion.

- A person who is put to death or endures great suffering on behalf of any belief, principle, or cause: a martyr to the cause of social justice.

Do either of those definitions describe Anne? No, they don't.

Also, Anne Boleyn did not risk her life by smuggling reformist books into England, her father, brother and chaplain did that.

Victim of Poison

What is it with Anne Boleyn and poison?! Despite Reformation. org's claim that Anne's miscarriages were caused by poison, there is absolutely no evidence that her miscarriages were anything but bad luck. The same site also claims that Catherine of Aragon's womb was closed by God to prevent her having male children as her marriage to Henry was incestuous. I applaud the site for its passion but it does not present any evidence for its wild claims.

A Sibyl or Prophetess

Another outrageous claim! For those of you who have not got a clue what a "sibyl", Dictionary.com defines a sibyl as

- Any of certain women of antiquity reputed to possess powers of prophecy or divination.

- A female prophet or witch.

As I have said, the radio show I heard about was claiming that Margaret of Austria ran a special school for gifted girls and women, for sibyls, and that Anne was one of those women. At

Margaret's school, Anne was also encouraged to fulfil her destiny and groomed to be Queen of England. Now, Anne Boleyn went to the court of Margaret of Austria in 1513, just 4 years after Henry's marriage to Catherine of Aragon and a time when Catherine was fertile and was getting pregnant. Obviously we are meant to think that as a sibyl Anne knew her destiny, but there was no hint then that Henry would give up Catherine. To me this claim is just way off base. What do you think?

Leader of the Reformation

Playwright Howard Brenton sees Anne Boleyn as a Joan of Arc type character and in his play he certainly does paint her as a brave reformer who changed English history.

Well, I agree that Anne had courage, that she had reformist views, that she owned books that could have got her condemned as a heretic, that she influenced the appointment of reformist bishops and that she had a genuine strong faith, but I would not say that she led the English Reformation or, as I heard someone claim, that she broke the Catholic Church in England. We also have to remember that Anne Boleyn was no Protestant. That label did not even exist then. She may have been a catalyst of the English Reformation and influenced Henry VIII with her 'heretical' reading material, but she was reformist rather than Protestant and she died in the Catholic faith. As my good friend, Olivia Peyton, said to me: 'Anne Boleyn did not want to throw the baby out with the bathwater', meaning that Anne could see that the Catholic Church was fundamentally ok, she did not reject the established religion and its rituals, but she realised that reform was required – the church needed some work!

Anne's almoner, John Skip, defended the ceremonies and rituals of the Catholic church in a sermon supported by Anne, defending them as aids to memory rather than the belief that they had sacred power. Eric Ives points out too that the reformist literature Anne was reading was not necessarily challenging the belief in transubstantiation, that Christ's body was present in the consecrated host, but instead was challenging the focus on the miracle rather than its meaning.

Eric Ives explains that Anne believed in real, personal spiritual experience, the priority of faith, the dissemination of the Bible and the reform of abuses in the Church, but that she did not hold heretical beliefs regarding the Host. She was an evangelical reformer not a radical.

Vampire

Do I really need to argue the case against this one? One recent vampire book had Anne Boleyn being hanged as obviously you cannot be a vampire if you have been decapitated. As much as I'd love to imagine Anne as a kick-ass vampire causing havoc in Tudor England, it's just not Anne is it? I love historical fiction and I love vampire novels but that doesn't mean that I love Tudor vampire books!

Conclusion

So, where does all this leave us? Who was the real Anne Boleyn? What was she really like?

Well, she didn't fit into any of the above labels and stereotypes! The real Anne Boleyn for me is the one Eric Ives describes so eloquently in his book "The Life and Death of Anne Boleyn". As I read about her background, her relationship with Henry, her reaction to the birth of Elizabeth, her love of fashion, art and culture, her strong faith, her downfall and the courage and dignity with which she faced her last days, I see glimpses of the real Anne Boleyn and begin to know her. She is a puzzle and always will be, she is an enigma and we will never know the entire truth about her, history won't let us, the sources are not there.

What we do know is that she wasn't an angel or a saint, but she also was not the devil incarnate. She was a woman who was passionate, intelligent, forward-thinking, hot-tempered, reckless at times and also quite spiteful. She didn't care what people thought of her ("let them grumble"), she tossed around empty threats and had a cruel streak (she ordered that Mary's ears be boxed if she didn't start toe-ing the line), she had heated arguments with her husband and was not afraid to question his judgement and disagree with him, she was jealous, she was insecure, she had reformist ideas but was not a radical.

Anne Boleyn is different things to different people and the puzzle of her story allows us to form her into what we want her to be and to love and admire her with a passion. Even today, she is causing arguments and heated debates, provoking strong reactions; and perhaps now, more than ever, inspiring people to write books and produce art and craft dedicated to her. She is like a modern day celebrity in that way, yet she lived over 450 years ago. Anne Boleyn is an icon.

Notes and Sources

- The Life and Death of Anne Boleyn, Eric Ives
- The Other Boleyn Girl, Philippa Gregory
- Harry Potter and the Philosopher's Stone, Warner Bros, 2001, based on the book by J K Rowling
- Rise and Growth of the Anglican Schism, Nicholas Sander
- Reformation.org
- The Spirit Revolution Radio Show, 2010, BBS Radio
- Divorced, Beheaded, Survived: A Feminist Reinterpretation of the Wives of Henry VIII, Karen Lindsey
- "Anne Boleyn, harlot or heroine? Was she a scheming sexual predator, or a brave reformer who changed Britain for ever?" – Article from The Daily Mail, 24th July 2010
- Anne Boleyn, Howard Brenton

Jane Seymour: The Meek and Mild One?

Jane Seymour has been rather neglected by authors and historians, probably because her relationship with Henry was rather short. Jane died around 17 months after her marriage to Henry. Many see her as a rather boring character. However, she is actually an interesting character and like all of Henry's wives she has been misrepresented and stereotyped.

Here are some of the labels, myths, opinions and stereotypes which surround Jane Seymour:-

- Jane was uneducated
- She was a 'plain Jane'
- Jane was meek, mild and demure
- Jane the virtuous and kind
- Jane the Peacemaker
- That Jane and Henry were betrothed at Wolf Hall and got married there
- Jane was much younger than Anne Boleyn
- That Jane was worse than Anne, in that she really did set out to trap Henry
- That Jane danced on Anne Boleyn's grave
- Jane came from a family of Catholic Conservatives
- Jane brought Henry's family together
- Jane was Henry's true love
- Jane died in childbirth
- Jane died as a result of an emergency caesarean and that Henry had to choose between her and the baby
- That Henry never planned to crown Jane
- Jane was pregnant when Henry married her and subsequently miscarried.

The Uneducated Wife?

Although Jane may not have received the same standard of education as her predecessors, Catherine of Aragon and Anne Boleyn, she received a traditional Tudor girl's education, which would have included subjects like needlework and music.[1] She would also have learned the 'art' of hunting. Eustace Chapuys, an enemy of Jane's predecessor, Anne Boleyn, described Jane as "not a woman of great wit, but she may have good understanding", so she may not have had the sharp mind of Anne Boleyn but she was far from thick and seems to have been blessed with common sense and an even temperament.

Jane's Appearance

Chapuys described Jane as "of middle stature and no great beauty, so fair that one would call her rather pale than otherwise"[2] and Alison Weir points out that Henry VIII was attracted to Jane not because of her physical looks but because she was different to Anne, she was her complete opposite. Anne had been a strong and ruthless character, whereas Jane was submissive and kind. Jane was chaste after the seemingly corrupt Anne.[3] Perhaps she reminded him of his mother, Elizabeth of York.

Holbein's portrait of Jane is far from flattering but we, today, have a very different idea about beauty. It is possible that the fair haired, pale skinned Jane was much closer to the Tudor idea of beauty, the English Rose, than the sallow-skinned, dark haired Anne Boleyn. To us, Jane looks dumpy, plain and rather chinless, to Henry she may have been a goddess!

Bound to Obey and Serve – Jane the Meek and Mild?

It is clear from Jane's motto that she wanted to be the submissive wife and queen, in contrast to the "Most Happy" Anne Boleyn who had a "sunshine and showers" relationship with Henry, one of passion and rages. Antonia Fraser describes Jane as being virtuous, sweet-natured and having common sense[4] and goes on to say that

Jane was the perfect Tudor woman, in comparison to the wayward Anne[5]. However, Alison Weir points out that lurking behind this mild mannered façade was a strong woman[6]. She may have been mild-mannered but she was capable of being strict with her household and also capable of standing up to her husband at times, although her common sense told her when to shut up. She listened to Henry when he threatened her, by reminding her of what had happened to wife number two, and learned to be submissive to her husband and master. Where Anne would have told Henry just what she thought, Jane curbed her tongue and accepted her place as the dutiful wife, but then she did have the benefit of knowing what Henry was capable of! Henry was bad-tempered and had mood swings and Jane was sensible enough to realise that he needed humouring and needed his ego massaging – where Anne could be impatient, Jane was soothing.

Jane the Virtuous and Kind

Although, when he first heard of Henry VIII's relationship with Jane, Chapuys wondered if she could really have reached the age of 25 at the English Court and have remained a virgin, it does seem that Jane was a truly chaste and virtuous woman. She has managed to reach her mid 20s without any scandal being attached to her name and when she was queen she carefully controlled her ladies and made sure that her household was known for its virtue.

Jane also seems to have been a kind woman and a woman who brought Henry happiness. In June 1536, Sir John Russell wrote to Lord Lisle saying:-

"The King came in his great boat to Greenwich that day with his privy chamber, and the Queen and the ladies in the great barge. I assure you she is as gentle a lady as ever I knew, and as fair a Queen as any in Christendom. "The King hath come out of hell into heaven for the gentleness in this and the cursedness and the unhappiness in the other." You would do well to write to the King again that you rejoice he is so well matched with so gracious a woman as is reported."[7]

Jane the Peacemaker

Although the Imperial Ambassador, Eustace Chapuys, had originally been rather scathing in regards to Henry's new love, describing her as "proud and haughty" and "not a woman of great wit", he soon changed his mind when he realised that she was sympathetic to the plight of the Lady Mary, daughter of Catherine of Aragon and Henry VIII. He then described Jane as a "pacific",[8] a peacemaker, and also praised her for her good sense and the way that she would not be drawn into discussions on religion and politics.

Wolf Hall

Wolf Hall may have been the Seymour family home and Jane may have retreated there after Anne Boleyn's execution,[9] but we know that Jane and Henry got betrothed at Hampton Court Palace and that their wedding took place in the Queen's closet at Whitehall, not Wolf Hall.

Jane's Age

Jane's exact birthdate is not known, but Elizabeth Norton points out that Jane had 29 ladies in her funeral procession in 1537, a lady for each year of her life.[10] Norton concludes that Jane was most likely born between October 1507 and October 1508. Jane was therefore around 28 when she married Henry VIII, and Chapuys describes her as "over 25 years old".[11] Obviously, there is controversy over Anne Boleyn's date of birth, with some historians saying 1501 and others 1507, but even if we take the 1501 birthdate for Anne then Jane was only six or seven years younger, although her family were known for their fertility.

Jane the Plotter and Seductress

Here we have the belief that Jane was not who she was cracked up to be, that she was coached, by Nicholas Carew,[12] in how to behave so that she attracted the King and kept his interest. She was encouraged to poison the King's mind against Anne Boleyn, while showing herself as an attractive alternative.[13] Her behaviour was all a well choreographed act.

Antonia Fraser[14] writes of how Jane refused to accept a gift of gold sovereigns from the king, flinging herself on her knees and begging the messenger to tell the king that she did not want to risk her honour. She asked the messenger to return the gift and to tell the King that she could only accept such a gift when she was married. This humble reaction inflamed the King's "ardour". Henry loved the thrill of the chase.

Was it part of a game, Jane's plan to ensnare the King? Had she learned from what had happened with Anne Boleyn? After all, Anne's rebuffing of the King had led to him pursuing her relentlessly and not taking no for an answer. Did Jane know what she was doing? Had she been coached on how to play the King by Carew and her brothers? Who knows? But Antonia Fraser does point out that it would have been characteristic for Jane to have acted in this way anyway and that it may not have been acting.[15]

It is easy for Anne Boleyn fans to accuse Jane of acting, of copying what Anne did, knowing how it had already worked on Henry. However, Jane is described by her contemporaries as being a genuinely humble, virtuous and chaste young woman. To refuse Henry's advances would have been natural for her to do. We cannot praise Anne for rebuffing Henry and challenge those who question Anne's motivations when, at the same time, we vilify Jane.

Did Jane Dance on Anne's Grave?

As I have said, there are those who believe that Jane took an active part in Anne's downfall by poisoning Henry's mind against his wife. Historian Agnes Strickland saw Jane as someone who coldly and mercilessly stood by, while her behaviour with Anne's husband led to Anne's miscarriage and ultimately Anne's death. Some imagine Jane as delighting in planning her marriage to Henry while Anne was imprisoned in the Tower waiting for the hour of her death, but just as Anne had no choice in marrying Henry, and we can't blame Anne for what happened to Catherine of Aragon, Jane had no choice in what happened either. Jane had loved and respected Catherine of Aragon and so probably did not have much respect for Anne Boleyn, but that does not mean that she took delight in what happened to Anne. She hardly danced on Anne's grave!

Jane the Catholic Queen

Although Jane's brothers Edward and Thomas Seymour later became staunch Protestants, and Edward was Lord Protector in the reign of the Protestant Edward VI (Jane's son), Jane was a conservative Catholic and Martin Luther described her as an "enemy of the gospel".[16]

Jane the Reconciler

Chapuys reported to Charles V how Jane, putting her characteristic meekness to one side, once pleaded with Henry VIII to restore the Lady Mary to the succession:-

"I hear that, even before the arrest of the Concubine, The King, speaking with mistress Jane [Seymour] of their future marriage, the latter suggested that the Princess should be replaced in her former position; and the King told her she was a fool, and ought to solicit the advancement of the children they would have between them, and not any others. She replied that in asking for the restoration of the Princess she conceived she was seeking the rest and tranquillity of the King, herself, her future children, and for the whole realm for without that, neither your Majesty nor his people would ever be content."[17]

It is clear from this exchange that Jane felt strongly about this issue as she continued pleading after Henry called her a fool. Alison Weir points out that however much Jane cared about reconciling Mary with her father, she showed no interest in Elizabeth and it was actually Mary's intercession which made Henry invite the little Elizabeth for the Christmas season of 1536/1537. Fraser contradicts this, saying that Jane fulfilled the role of a benevolent mother to both girls, although she points out that Jane could not have reconciled the King with his daughters if Henry really did not want to be.[18.]

Henry's True Love

Henry VIII called Jane his true love and true wife. He chose Jane's image to be portrayed as his wife and queen in the Whitehall Family Portrait, even though he was married to Catherine Parr at the time. He also chose to be laid to rest next to Jane, so it is hard to argue with that and say that she was not Henry's true love. But he was only involved with Jane for around 18 months, if that, so the relationship cannot be compared with his marriage to Catherine of Aragon, which lasted for nearly 24 years, or his relationship with Anne Boleyn, which lasted about 10 years. Henry did not have time to get tired of Jane and the fact that she died after giving him the precious gift of a son probably made Henry look back on their relationship with rather rose tinted spectacles! There is no doubt, however, that he loved and respected her and his behaviour after her death, locking himself away from the world, shows that he really was grief-stricken.

The Birth of Edward VI, Jane's son

Jane Seymour went into labour on the 9th October 1537 and her labour lasted for three days and three nights. Alison Weir writes of how there were rumours that doctors stretched her arms and legs to ease the delivery of the baby and that Henry was asked whether he wanted to save Jane or the baby. Allegedly, he chose the child because he could easily find another wife, so a caesarean section was then performed. There is absolutely no evidence that any of that happened and there is no way that Jane would have survived the ordeal had she undergone a caesarean section.

The new prince was finally born at 2am on the 12th Oct 1537. Jane was well enough to receive the christening guests in her apartments on the 15th October but suffered an attack of diarrhoea on the afternoon of the 16th and started to be sick that night. She rapidly went downhill and was given the last rites on the 17th. However, she then seemed to improve, so much so that Henry continued the christening celebrations.

The puerperal fever was not gone though and on Friday 19th Jane became feverish once more and slipped into delirium. Contrary to popular opinion, Henry was very worried about his wife. Alison Weir writes that he had intended to return to Esher for the beginning of the hunting season but he put this off because he wanted to be near Jane. On the evening of the 23rd, Henry was summoned to Jane's bedside as it was obvious that she was dying. Weir writes of how he remained with her that night and that she died in the early hours of the 24th October. Henry was devastated and hid himself away at Windsor, refusing to see anyone. He wallowed for 3 weeks and wore full mourning for 3 months after Jane's death. His happiness at the birth of his much longed for son had been eclipsed by the death of his wife and queen. It was a few months before Henry could bring himself to do his duty and look for another wife.

Jane as Queen

Jane was only queen for a short time but she had shown what kind of queen she hoped to be.[19] It was clear that she intended to stay Henry's wife and queen and that she modelled herself on Catherine of Aragon, Henry's first wife. She aimed to provide Henry with a son and heir, to reconcile the King and his daughter Mary, and to advance the Seymours at court. Weir comments that Jane achieved pretty much everything that she had set out to do:-

- She provided the King with a son and heir
- She helped reconcile Mary and Henry and helped to restore the Lady Mary to the succession
- She advanced her family
- She provided the King with a stable family life
- She submitted to the King, obeyed him and did not meddle with things like religion and politics which did not concern her, after being reprimanded when she did speak to Henry about the monasteries.

Was Jane pregnant before her marriage to Henry?

Although in one fictional account of Anne Boleyn's downfall (I think it was Jean Plaidy's "Murder Most Royal"), Jane becomes pregnant, there is no evidence that this happened in real life. It seems that Jane was a virgin until her wedding night.

Jane's Planned Coronation

Although Henry may have been once bitten and twice shy (or actually twice bitten!), as in he had forked out for two coronations already, he did plan to have Jane crowned queen and payments for preparations for her coronation are recorded in the royal accounts. Her coronation was originally planned for September/October 1536 and was only postponed due to an outbreak of the plague. In 1537, Jane became pregnant and I suspect that Henry then held off crowning her due to her condition, planning to go ahead with the ceremony after she had recovered from the birth.

Conclusion

Having researched Jane Seymour and having read contemporary accounts of her behaviour as Henry's wife and queen, I have to take her at face value and believe that she really was the sweet, virtuous, kind woman that she made herself out to be - either that or she was an incredibly good actress! I do believe that she was coached by Carew and her brothers but I don't think that she had to act, I think her behaviour was natural. As much as I'd love to believe that she had a dark side, I don't believe she had one. She really was a virtuous woman through and through and cannot be held accountable for what happened to Anne Boleyn, just as Anne cannot be held accountable for what happened to Catherine of Aragon. Jane made Henry happy, she gave him the gift of a son, she was a peacemaker, she was popular with the people and she was a humble, kind woman. It's just a shame that her time as queen was so short-lived.

Notes and Sources

1. Jane Seymour: Henry VIII's True Love, Elizabeth Norton, p12

2. LP x.901

3. The Six Wives of Henry VIII, Alison Weir

4. The Six Wives of Henry VIII, Antonia Fraser, p290

5. Ibid.

6. Alison Weir

7. LP x.1047

8. LP x.1069

9. Fraser, p317

10. Norton, p11

11. LP x.901

12. Calendar of State Papers, Spain, Volume 5 Part 2: 1536-1538, 1888, pp. 104-118.

13. The Life and Death of Anne Boleyn, Eric Ives, p304

14. Fraser, p295

15. Ibid., p296

16. Ibid., p334

17. LP x.908

18. Fraser, p331-332

19. Alison Weir

Anne of Cleves – Flanders Mare?

Anne of Cleves seems to have gone down in history as the ugly one, the Flanders Mare who Henry found so unattractive that he just couldn't bring himself to consummate their union. But what other opinions, labels, myths and stereotypes are there out there about Henry VIII's fourth wife?:-

- Anne of Cleves the Flanders Mare
- That she smelled bad
- That she was not a virgin
- That Anne was a strict Lutheran
- Anne had no fashion sense
- She had children with Henry VIII
- She hoped to remarry Henry after the fall of Catherine Howard
- Anne was already pre-contracted to someone else
- That she had a lesbian affair with Catherine Howard
- Anne of Cleves was the one who got away and outlived them all
- Anne had royal blood
- Anne of Cleves was half-horse and half-human

So, let's look at these statements one by one and see what the real truth about Anne of Cleves is...

Anne of Cleves the Flanders Mare

Although Anne of Cleves has gone down in history as the Flanders Mare, the wife who was ugly and looked like a horse, it is only Henry VIII who seems to have considered her ugly. In January 1539, Henry VIII sent Christopher Mont, a member of Thomas Cromwell's household, as ambassador to Germany to discuss a possible marriage between the Princess Mary and William, Anne of Cleves' brother, and to investigate the daughters of the Duke of Cleves. He wanted to know about their looks, education and qualities.[1] Mont reported back that everyone praised Anne's beauty and that she was even more beautiful than the renowned European beauty, the Duchess of Milan. He was going on hearsay, though, as he had not seen Anne himself.

In March 1539, Henry sent ambassadors to Cleves to get further reports on Anne and to get a portrait, but the ambassadors encountered difficulties as Anne and her sister kept their faces covered. In the summer of 1539, Henry sent his court painter, Hans Holbein, to Cleves to paint Anne and her younger sister. When the leading English ambassador, Nicholas Wotton, saw Holbein's portraits of the sisters, he declared that the artist had captured the ladies' liknesses[2] and that others also considered the portraits a good likeness of the young women. Although we do not know what Henry thought of Anne from her portrait, we have to conclude that he liked what he saw as he continued with negotiations. Why then did the King take an instant dislike to his bride-to-be when he first encountered her at Rochester on New Year's Day 1540? Why did he adamantly declare "I like her not"?

In my opinion, Henry was humiliated and embarrassed by their first meeting, which had been a complete disaster. Always the romantic, Henry had decided to surprise Anne by disguising himself in the great chivalric tradition and intercepting her on her way to London. According to this tradition, the would-be bride would see through the disguise, fall in love at first sight and swoon into her beloved's arms. It would be the perfect first date and they would both live happily ever after. Unfortunately, Anne knew nothing of this tradition, did not recognise Henry and was shocked and scared by this monstrous man who tried to embrace her and take such liberties with her. She acted in an entirely proper way but she failed to recognise Henry for who he was and failed to react in the way that Henry had anticipated.

We don't know whether Anne lived up to her portrait, but I

think it was her reaction to Henry which sealed her fate. If she had been ugly then why did nobody else notice and why did Holbein risk painting her the way he did? Of course, it could be that Anne with her tall stature, her rather long nose and heavy lidded eyes was just very different to Henry's previous wives, perhaps she just wasn't Henry's type.

Contrary to legend, there is no evidence that Anne wore a huge blonde wig and that she was actually dark-haired, or that she was dark-skinned or "swarthy".

Did Anne of Cleves Smell Bad?

On the morning after their wedding night, Henry VIII made it clear that he did not like Anne and claimed that she was smelly.[3] Hmm... a rather hypocritical comment coming from a man with a nasty leg ulcer which often smelled to high heaven!

Henry expected perfection and perhaps Anne did suffer with body odour or perhaps she used a scent which Henry just did not like. Of course, Henry had already made up his mind that he did not like her before the wedding night and had felt pushed into the marriage. I can just picture Henry having a tantrum on the morning of the 7th of January and acting like a child, "I said I didn't like her and I still don't", or words to that effect!

Was Anne of Cleves a Virgin?

Of course the poor girl was! Anne seems to have been a complete innocent and completely ignorant of what sexual intercourse involved. So much so that it appears that she thought she had done her duty by kissing the King goodnight! However, Henry professed on the morning after that Anne could not possibly be a maid due to her having 'loose' breasts.[4] Perhaps Anne was simply large breasted, who knows? But Henry was not satisfied with her body. Henry had found Anne so unattractive that he had not been able to have sex with her. He told his physicians how Anne's body just did not excite him.[5] In other words, Anne's appearance had led to Henry not being able "to get it up", something which, of course, could not possibly be Henry's fault! After all, he had experienced wet dreams and thought that he would be able to have sex with others – yeah, right! Anyway, Henry later annulled his marriage on various grounds, including non-consummation, so Anne did not lose her maidenhead to the King.

Anne of Cleves the Lutheran Queen

Although Alison Weir writes of how Henry VIII's daughter, Mary, was shocked that her father was marrying someone she regarded as a heretic[6] and how Mary helped to convert Anne to Catholicism, I'm not sure that Anne of Cleves was a staunch Protestant.

Elizabeth Norton, in her biography of Anne, points out that Anne's religious education was controlled by her mother, a devout Catholic, and that her father was humanist rather than Lutheran. He had reformist sympathies, but he was still a Catholic.[7] Later in her book, Norton goes on to say that Anne must have conformed to the reformed faith in Edward VI's time because there is no reference to her religion during his reign. However, she was prominent at court in the early years of Mary I's reign, she was happy to attend mass and it appears that she died in the Catholic faith.[8] Perhaps Anne the pragmatist just did what she could to survive, perhaps her beliefs were those of a 'reformed' Catholic, someone sitting on the fence, and so she was happy to abide by the law of the land.

Anne the Frumpy Queen

It's not so much that Anne of Cleves was a frump and had no dress sense, it's just that her dress was very different to English dress at that time. Elizabeth Norton points out that Anne was used to the heavier fashions of Germany and the Low Countries,[9] a style that was very different to that of England and which was not at all flattering. Holbein's portratit of her shows her in a headdress which was very different to the English gable hood favoured by

Jane Seymour or the French hood favoured by Anne Boleyn.

Children and Remarriage?

Once when I wrote about Anne of Cleves, a gentleman called "Prince of England and Ireland from Tudor-Cleves Ludovit Bialon" wrote to me advising me that he was descended from Anne of Cleves and Henry VIII through a princess who was born to them in Autumn 1540. Unfortunately, according to Ludovit, Anne's children had to be sent into exile, to Hungary, where their descendants still live today.

Now, King of Gossip, Eustace Chapuys, wrote in December 1541 that Anne of Cleves "was known to have gone away in the family way from the King, and had actually been confined this summer",[10] but there is no evidence to back up this rumour and although it appears that Anne expected to be re-instated as Henry's wife and queen after the fall of Catherine Howard, Henry was not inclined to take her back. Ludovit cited two sources in his email to me but the first one was simply a report by Chapuys of Anne and Henry's meeting on New Year's Day, and it definitely would not have been proper for the King and Queen to sleep together before their official marriage ceremony. The second source he cited was Agnes Strickland, but I cannot find any mention of any document in Agnes Strickland's book regarding the birth of a child to Anne. Gossip and rumour is what this all boils down to and if Henry had had a son by Anne he certainly would have recognised him in some way.

The Pre-Contract

One of the issues used as grounds for the annulment of Henry VIII's marriage to Anne of Cleves was the alleged pre-contract between Anne and Francis of Lorraine. Anne's betrothal to Francis, heir of the Duke of Lorraine, had been arranged by her father in 1527 but was broken when Anne's brother, who became Duke of Jülich-Cleves-Berg on the death of his father in 1538, refused to give up the territory of Guelders to the Duke of Lorraine in 1539. Henry VIII's Council had looked into the issue of the betrothal in January 1540, when Henry was trying to wriggle out of marrying Anne, but Anne's brother's ambassadors had been able to ensure the Council that Anne was free to marry and that the betrothal had been abandoned many years before. In February 1540, the ambassadors had been able to provide the Council with a notarial certificate stating that the betrothal had been broken off as early as 1535, although the original documents no longer existed.

Anne of Cleves and Catherine Howard

I have not yet read Brandy Purdy's novel, "The Boleyn Wife", but I have heard that there is a lesbian 'encounter' between Anne of Cleves and Catherine Howard. I have also seen discussions online pondering whether the non-consummation between Anne and Henry was because Anne was actually a lesbian. Now, just because Anne did not sleep with Henry it does not mean that she was a lesbian and just because she is depicted as having a lesbian fling with Catherine Howard in a novel it does not mean that it happened in real life!

The Survivor and the One Who Got Away

Anne of Cleves managed to get out of her marriage to Henry with her head held high (and still connected to her neck, a feat in itself!), property and money, the title of "right dear and right entirely beloved sister" and a good relationship with the King and his children. She also outlived Henry and his other wives, dying on the 15th July 1557 (although she was only 41). So, she can be seen as the one who survived, the one who got away, the lucky one. BUT I wonder if she was really happy. Elizabeth Norton writes of how Anne always believed herself to be Henry's true wife and queen but she knew that she had to deny her feelings to survive.[11]

She sacrificed a part of herself when she submitted to Henry's request for an annulment and I wonder if money and status really made up for what she lost, the chance of marriage and children. It's hard to say.

Royal Blood

Like all of Henry's wives, and Henry himself, Anne of Cleves was descended from Edward I. But Anne was also descended from the French Kings, being related to Louis XII of France on her father's side.

Half-horse and half-human

When I was researching myths about Anne of Cleves, I actually stumbled on someone asking "Was anne of cleves half horse and half human?" on Wiki Answers.com! Someone had answered, saying "No, no she was not", thankfully! I'm glad that we managed to sort that one out!

Notes and Sources

1. Anne of Cleves: Henry VIII's Discarded Bride, Elizabeth Norton, p31
2. Ibid., p36
3. The Six Wives of Henry VIII, Alison Weir, p382
4. Ibid.
5. Six Wives: The Queens of Henry VIII, David Starkey
6. Weir, p367
7. Norton, p11
8. Norton, p146
9. Norton, p71
10. LP xvi. 1441
11. Norton, p112

Catherine Howard – The Material Girl?

Catherine Howard has been on my mind a lot over the past few weeks, due to the BBC finally airing the final season of "The Tudors". I've been struggling to understand her and how she got into the almighty mess that saw her go from the King's "jewel of womanhood" to being executed as a traitor and adulteress. Catherine is like her cousin, Anne Boleyn, in many ways, a bit of an enigma.

So, before we try to get to grips with who the fifth wife of Henry VIII really was, let's look at the labels she has been given and the way she has been represented in fiction and on TV:-

- Rose without a thorn – Henry VIII referred to Catherine as his "Rose without a thorn" and "a jewel of womanhood".

- Victim of child abuse and paedophiles – The idea that Catherine was preyed on by her music teacher and three older men: Dereham, the King and Culpeper.

- Slut, prostitute and common harlot – The Tudors Season 3 episode guide describes Catherine as a "prostitute" and the series shows Charles Brandon, Duke of Suffolk, and Edward Seymour, Earl Hertford, procuring Catherine and almost pimping her out to the King.

- Romantic heroine – The Victorians saw Catherine as a tragic, romantic heroine forced into marriage with a fat, smelly tyrant, but who was in love with a dashing courtier.

- A teenage tearaway – The idea that Catherine lacked a proper upbringing and that she was allowed to run riot in the busy household of the Dowager Duchess of Norfolk and was corrupted by the behaviour of her elders there.

- Airhead and bimbo – Catherine is often seen as an airhead and bimbo, a girl whose only education consisted of how to please a man. This was emphasised by the giggly and dizzy character of Catherine in "The Tudors".

- Material Girl – A true material girl who loved jewels, pretty dresses, money etc. and who thought of nothing else.

- A tragic character looking for love, attention and affection – The idea that Catherine had been starved of love in her childhood and was just looking for love and attention, and that's why she had her dalliance with Thomas Culpeper.

- A victim of manipulative older men – Some portray Catherine as putty in the hands of older men who used her and abused her.

- A reckless fool – That Catherine was a giddy girl who could easily lose her head over a man.[1]

- Always naked – Did anyone else notice that Catherine Howard spent most of her time naked in The Tudors? Naked on a swing, naked practising with the block, naked except for rose petals...

- A nymphomaniac – A promiscuous girl who put her sexual desires ahead of everything else.

- Cold, calculating and ambitious - The Catherine Howard of Suzannah Dunn's "The Confession of Katherine Howard". Kate as she is called in that, seemed to be a girl who used people to get to the top and who used Culpeper to try and provide the King with an heir.

- Spoilt child – Was Catherine just a self-indulgent teenager used to getting her own way and used to getting away with things because she was pretty and plump?[2]

- A Proud Howard – A girl whose Howard pride cost her her life.

- A worldly girl – The idea that Catherine was very worldly wise and sexually experienced, that she even knew methods of contraception. Michael Hirst describes her as a "Lolita figure".

Catherine Howard's Age

Many of the above labels and views depend on how old you think Catherine was when she had her relationships with Henry Manox, Francis Dereham, Henry VIII and Thomas Culpeper, so when was Catherine Howard born?

That is a very tricky question to answer and historians argue over this just as they do over Anne Boleyn's birth date. Lacey Baldwin Smith devotes the appendix[3] of his book, "Catherine Howard", to this question. In it, he cites the various clues we have:-

- The will of Dame Isabel Legh, Catherine's maternal grandmother – Catherine is mentioned in this will from 1527 so she was definitely born before 1527.

- The will of John Legh, Isabel's husband and Catherine's step-grandfather – This will from 1524 does not mention Catherine and although some historians use this as proof that Catherine was not born until after 1524, Baldwin Smith points out that it also does not mention any of the Howard girls. He argues that baby girls may not have warranted a mention in wills, they weren't seen as important.[4]

- That if Catherine's parents, Jocasta Culpeper and Edmund Howard, married around 1514-1515, as has been suggested, and Catherine had three elder brothers, then Catherine could not have been born before 1517/1518.

- The French Ambassador reported that Catherine was 18 years of age when she slept with Francis Dereham[5] and that Catherine's confession dated their affair to 1538-1539. However, the ambassador also said that Dereham had been involved in a sexual relationship with her when she was between 13 and 18. If Catherine was 18 in 1539 then her year of birth would be 1521.

- The Spanish Chronicle (The Chronicle of Henry VIII) has Catherine meeting the King at the age of 15, making her date of birth 1524.

- The Toledo Museum portrait of Catherine Howard – Lacey Baldwin Smith writes of how this portrait gives Catherine's age as 21 and was painted c1540/1541 – However, some historians do not believe that this portrait is of Catherine.

Lacey Baldwin Smith does say that all of this is speculation and many things, including her parents' marriage date, are "conjectural". All we really know for sure about Catherine's family is that Edward Howard said that he was the father of ten children in 1527. We are left none-the-wiser, with Catherine being anything from 11 to 15 when Manox had a relationship with her, and 17 to 21 when she died.

Catherine Howard's Appearance

We only have one definite likeness of Catherine Howard and that is the miniature by Hans Holbein. David Starkey[6] writes of how we can be sure that this is Catherine because she can be identified by the jewels she is wearing, which match with contemporary records of jewels she owned at the time. This miniature shows a young woman with an English rose complexion, auburn hair, dark eyes and the start of a double chin. Starkey also describes her as pretty and plump. Joanna Denny describes Catherine as being blonde with a "peaches-and-cream complexion".[7] Later, in her book, Denny writes of Catherine's hazel coloured eyes[8] and her love of French fashion with its low cut necklines which often exposed the breasts! No wonder that Henry noticed her!

Antonia Fraser[9] writes of how the French Ambassador rated her beauty as just "middling", which, interestingly, was how he had also described Anne of Cleves, and she was also described by contemporaries as petite and diminutive. She must have looked tiny compared to the King who was over six feet tall and had a chest measurement of 57 inches and a waist measurement of 54 inches in 1541.

Victim of Child Abuse

As I said, the way we view Catherine's life and what happened to her does depend on what birthdate we accept for her, but, we have to remember that Tudor girls went from being a child to being a woman. There weren't teenagers in Tudor times. Joanna Denny writes of how, today, Manox's relationship with Catherine would be viewed as child abuse, however, girls were seen as sexually mature and ready for marriage at the onset of puberty.[10]

Lacey Baldwin Smith explains that child marriages were the norm in the Tudor area and comments that Catherine's own mother had married at 12.[11] We know that Henry VIII's grandmother was 12 when she married and 13 when she gave birth. If we accept the 1521 birthdate, as Lacey Baldwin Smith and David Starkey do, then Catherine was around 14/15 when Manox and she were involved, and around 19 when she married the King. Although Manox, Dereham, Culpeper, and particularly Henry VIII, were older than her, it was not unusual for a young woman to be involved with an older man. Charles Brandon, Duke of Suffolk, had married his ward, Catherine Willoughby, when she was just 13/14 and he was in his late 40s.

Slut, Prostitute and Common Harlot

As I said earlier, the episode guide to "The Tudors" Season 3 described Catherine as a prostitute and it certainly portrayed her as sexually experienced. We see her seducing Henry, something that does not tally with his perception of her as virginal, and we also know that she has had experience with other men, she has a rather colourful past.

It is true. Catherine Howard had been involved to some extent with Henry Manox and Francis Dereham before her marriage to Henry VIII. Manox had boasted to Mary Hall (née Mary Lascelles), one of the women in the Dowager Duchess's household, that he knew Catherine intimately, that he had had her "by the cunt" and that she had promised him her "maidenhead".[12] Manox also said that he knew a "privy mark" in Catherine's "secret parts",[13] but it seems that the couple did not 'go all the way' as when he was questioned later, he was adamant that he had never actually had full sexual intercourse with her. It seems that it was Dereham who de-flowered the "rose without a thorn".

According to Joanna Denny,[14] Francis Dereham was a gentleman of the Duke of Norfolk and a favourite of the Dowager Duchess. He and other young men in the Norfolk household sneaked into the Maidens' Chamber, the girls' dormitory, at night, enjoying sexual relations with the females there. He had previously had a relationship with Catherine's friend and dormitory companion, Joan Bulmer, but was soon taken with Catherine. The couple obviously had a full sexual relationship because Catherine's bed companion, Alice Restwood, described "puffing and blowing" between the couple. Another witness, Mary Lascelles, testified that "they would kiss and hang by their bills [lips] together and [as if] they were two sparrows" Margaret Benet described how she saw Dereham pull Catherine's clothes up so that he could see her private parts[15].

Although these illicit goings-on went on by night at the Dowager Duchess's homes in Horsham and Lambeth, Antonia Fraser points out that it could not be likened to a brothel, it was more of a posh finishing school.[16] Catherine Howard was not a prostitute in a brothel and her affair with Manox can be put down to youthful experimentation. Her relationship with Dereham could have been described as a marriage, in that the couple had agreed to marry. They referred to each other as husband and wife and they had consummated the relationship. Although Catherine went on to have secret meetings with Thomas Culpeper, her husband's groom, and evidently planned to sleep with him, I'm not sure that she can be labelled as promiscuous or a slut, more a girl who lacked judgement and loved attention.

Romantic Heroine

It is tempting to feel sorry for Catherine, to see her as a teenage beauty who's had a rough upbringing, starved of love and affection. A girl forced into a loveless marriage (on her side anyway) with a monster and who can't help but have an affair with the love of her life: the swashbuckling, gorgeous Thomas Culpeper. Hmm... tempting, but it's not what happened in real life, is it?

OK, so Catherine's mother died when she was young and she had an absent father, but she was sent to stay with family and she was no different from many girls of her age and station. She had friends, she had fun, and then she ended up in the glamorous world of the English Court, serving the new queen, Anne of Cleves. There she met Thomas Culpeper, who was far from the romantic hero of chivalric legend. He was a man who Antonia Fraser describes as more like Don Giovanni than the romantic hero Lancelot. In fact, he was a rapist and murderer, and was quick to lay the blame on Catherine and Lady Rochford when he was caught out. Catherine married a man who doted on her. The King gave her everything she wanted, including love and affection, and she cheated on him. The furious King had his "Desdemona"[17] executed, along with her love and previous lover, and that was the end of little Catherine Howard.

The romantic Catherine and Culpeper story comes from the pages of The Spanish Chronicle[18] which tells of how the couple fell in love before Catherine's wedding to the King, that Culpeper "was much grieved and fell very ill" when Catherine married Henry VIII and that "every time he went to the palace and saw the Queen he did nothing but sigh, and by his eyes let the Queen know what trouble he was suffering". Catherine was then tempted by the Devil and "as Culpepper was a gentleman and young, and the King was old, she remembered the good-will she formerly bore to the young courtier, and let him know by signs that he might cheer up." It goes on to tell how the couple corresponded by letter and that Catherine bribed Jane Rochford with dresses, jewels and the promise of an

honourable marriage to keep her secret and to help her meet with
Culpeper. Jane apparently betrayed Catherine by telling the Duke
of Somerset (who wasn't even Duke of Somerset at this time!).
Culpeper was arrested and interrogated by Cromwell (who was
dead by this time!) and others. In this romanticised version of
the story, Culpeper and Catherine have done nothing but write
to each other. Culpeper does not lay the blame on Catherine and
instead talks of his love for the Queen, "the thing I loved best in
the world... though you may hang me for it". When Catherine is
executed, in this account, she says to the crowd "I die a Queen, but
I would rather die the wife of Culpepper!" How romantic! But can
we really rely on this overly romanticised account with all of its
inaccuracies? I doubt it.

In my opinion, Catherine was far from the romantic heroine
and the story is far from a fairytale, chivalric legend or romantic
tragedy. It is a sordid story of ambition, lust, lies, power and
downright foolishness.

Teenage Tearaway, Spoilt Child and Immature Airhead?

As I have said, teenagers did not really exist in Tudor times,
but, it is easy to see Catherine as a spoilt child. Like a child saying
"I want, I want..." all the time and sticking out her bottom lip and
sulking if she didn't get her way. That is certainly the Catherine of
"The Tudors", the young woman who confronts her step-daughter,
Mary, hands on hips, accusing her, in quite a whiny voice, of not
showing her the respect she is due as queen. When Mary does
not play ball and accuses Catherine of being frivolous, Catherine
removes two of Mary's ladies and draws attention to Mary's single
status. When Mary says "How dare you speak to me like that?",
Catherine replies "I dare because I can!" Isn't that something that a
teenage girl would say in an argument? It's an incredibly immature
reply.

Lacey Baldwin Smith describes Catherine as being a cheerful

girl who had no idea that her actions could have such serious consequences. She was like a pampered girl who expected to get what she wanted and who sulked if she didn't. Unfortunately, her behaviour seems to have been encouraged.[19] However, David Starkey sees a different side of Catherine, commenting on her leadership qualities and "resourcefulness".[20]

Starkey writes of how Catherine was quick to form a good relationship with Archbishop Thomas Cranmer, showing her intelligence. She acted graciously when her predecessor, Anne of Cleves, visited Court and she was kind, loving and good-natured. She may not have had the intelligence of her predecessors or their strong faith, but she seems to have been a likable girl who managed to get on with her stepdaughter Mary, who doted on the Princess Elizabeth and who was loyal to those she'd grown up with and who were her friends. While she may have been foolish in giving Francis Dereham the position of her private secretary, and her former bedfellows positions as her ladies, it shows that she was a caring person. Starkey writes of how she wasn't a martyr but she was not cruel and did not make martyrs of others.[21] She had character traits that can be admired.

Rather than being a failure as queen, Starkey believes that she had actually made a good start as consort and writes that she was clever in combining Jane Seymour's submissive character, in her motto "no other wish but his", with the style of Anne Boleyn.[22] It is such as shame that this queen who showed such promise, and who obviously had the affection of her husband, could not control her feelings.

I should also point out that although she was not highly educated, Catherine was literate, as is shown from her letter to Thomas Culpeper. She may have put jewels and pretty dresses before learning, but she was not thick and her level of education could be compared to the likes of Jane Seymour. I think "The Tudors" lets Catherine down when it portrays her as a girl who spent all of her time "oohing" at pretty things, laughing at the book of midwifery and giggling more than talking.

The Material Girl

There's no denying that Catherine Howard was a material girl. For a girl who had grown up in a kind of boarding school, sharing a bed with another girl and not having any possessions to really call her own, it must have been a dream come true to become queen and to be lavished with jewels, dresses, money, property etc. Joanna Denny writes that even before the annulment of his marriage to Anne of Cleves Henry was showering his new love with gifts of jewels and gowns[23]. Marillac, the French ambassador, wrote of how the King spent more money on her than on any of his previous wives.[24]

Lacey Baldwin Smith describes her a fun loving, "giddy" girl, but who can blame her for enjoying herself and making the most of the King's attentions, wouldn't you at her age?

A Naked Nymphomaniac

I had to laugh in "The Tudors" when they showed a naked Catherine practising with the block on the night before her execution! I think my comment to my husband was "Oh, another opportunity to show her naked!". She did seem to be naked or partially dressed most of the time in the series! When you combine this with the stories of her past in Horsham and Lambeth, her seduction of Henry VIII and her illicit meetings with Thomas Culpeper, it is easy to imagine Catherine as a complete nympho. Also, was it me, or was there a hint that she hadn't just had experience with men? Wasn't there a bit when Joan Bulmer was stroking her bare shoulder in bed? Hmm...

The Catherine Howard I believe in was not a nymphomaniac, she was simply a young and passionate woman who fell head over heels in love with the wrong man at the wrong time. It is clear from the letter that was found in Culpeper's belongings that she was completely besotted with him. We have all known women who have fallen hopelessly in love with the wrong man, with a bad boy, and who have lived to regret it. Poor Catherine was not so lucky.

A Worldly Girl

Catherine Howard grew up quickly in the household of the Dowager Duchess of Norfolk. She had been 'corrupted' by seeing the sexual behaviour of older girls and boys, and having her own dalliances with older boys. It is ironic that the wife who Henry referred to as his "rose without a thorn" was the one who was far from virginal and who even boasted that "a woman might meddle with a man and yet conceive no child unless she would herself". She obviously had some knowledge of the primitive contraception of the age, even if it was simply coitus interruptus.

David Starkey makes the point that Henry, who had struggled to 'get it up' (sorry to sound so vulgar but I'm not quite sure how else to put it!) with Anne of Cleves, had no problem with Catherine and there are many reports of him not being able to keep his hands off her even in public. Starkey goes on to say Henry was too caught up in the excitement to question where she got her love-making skills from. Did Henry never wonder how his wife knew so much about sex and pleasuring her man? Could this 'whore in the bedroom' really be a virgin? Perhaps he just pushed his doubts to one side because he was so desperate to be happy and to have another son.

A Proud Howard

Catherine Howard was a member of the powerful Howard family. Although she was one of the less important Howards, being the daughter of Edmund Howard, third son of Thomas Howard, 2nd Duke of Norfolk, she definitely had the Howard pride.

When Archbishop Thomas Cranmer interviewed Catherine regarding the allegations that she had had a carnal relationship with Francis Dereham, Catherine begged for the King's forgiveness and mercy but would not admit to there being any type of pre-contract or marriage between the two of them. Her pride prevented her from seeing that admitting to being pre-contracted to Dereham could save her. With the benefit of hindsight, we can see that Catherine's life may have been spared if she had confessed to the pre-contract as her marriage to Henry could then have been annulled on these grounds. If only she had been willing to put her pride and title aside, then Dereham may not have been tortured, Culpeper's name may not have come up, and she may have kept her head. It was the Howard pride that made Catherine fight to stay queen.[25]

An Innocent Victim of a Manipulative Man?

One thing I am not sure about is whether Catherine Howard was the victim of a manipulative man, a man with a plan. It is clear that Thomas Culpeper had a dark side and a sordid past. After his arrest and execution, a merchant in London wrote to a friend in Germany of how, two years previously to his execution, Culpeper had raped a park-keeper's wife while his companions held her down.[26] The merchant went on to say that Culpeper killed a man when an attempt was made to apprehend him for the crime, but that he was pardoned for the crimes by the King. It seems that Culpeper had grown up at court and Joanna Denny writes of how his good looks and his skills at dressing Henry VIII's ulcerous leg had led to him being a favourite. Indeed, he slept in the King's chamber and, according to the French ambassador, may even have shared the King's bed.[27]

Although Culpeper had this rather colourful past, he was also very popular at court. Lady Lisle sent him a hawk, notes and various gifts and Joanna Denny describes how women found him attractive. David Starkey writes of him being popular with men and women due to his good looks and charm. He was the proverbial 'bad boy', the type of man who some women feel the need to tame.

Catherine, according to Starkey, was "his female equivalent" and he goes on to say that when Catherine first got to court it was rumoured that she and Culpeper would marry, but then they drifted apart and she married the King. What is not clear is whether Culpeper set out to win Catherine back in order to benefit from her status or from her future status. As a man who was close to the King, who dressed the King's leg ulcer, he would have known about the two flare ups of the infection in 1541, both of which were serious and thought to be life threatening. Did Culpeper believe that the King was not long for this world and did he think that he could control the Dowager Queen Catherine and therefore also the new King, if Catherine was made regent? Who knows? But the trusting, kindly and young Catherine could have been easy prey for Culpeper.

Catherine the Fool?

I really disagree with comments suggesting that Catherine deserved her fate as I don't believe that anyone deserves to die such a brutal death, however, I have to conclude that Catherine was incredibly stupid and foolhardy. I cannot blame her for keeping her past a secret, after all, at what point do you say to the rather moody Henry VIII "by the way, darling, I'm not a virgin"? Plus, Catherine probably thought that her past was firmly behind her, she had no way of knowing that Dereham would come back from Ireland and end up on her doorstep. But, she must have had rocks in her head to believe that she could have secret meetings with Thomas Culpeper and get away with it. Did she not remember what had happened to her cousin just a few years before!

Historians such as Lacey Baldwin Smith talk about how Catherine would have seen examples of other women, such as Dorothy Bray (a lady in waiting), taking a lover at court. But they weren't the Queen were they? It may have been exciting to have a dashing young man in love with you and it may have been highly tempting to take things further when your husband just didn't do it for you, but surely Catherine was well aware of the danger of acting on such an impulse. There is no doubt in my mind, that she was foolish and reckless.

What we don't know is whether anyone tried to stop her. Surely one of her ladies should have pulled her to one side and said "What are you doing? Don't be stupid! Look at what happened to Anne Boleyn?" Perhaps one of them did and Catherine was too head over heels in love to take any notice, perhaps she was blinded by love and passion and thought she could get away with it. Or, perhaps she was let down by those who were older and should have known better.

Cold and Calculating?

The Kate of Suzannah Dunn's novel is desperate to get pregnant by any means. When her friend, Cat, worries about her relationship with Culpeper and a possible pregnancy, Kat laughs and says that she actually needs to get pregnant.[28] Although this seems a good reason for Catherine's rather reckless relationship with Thomas Culpeper, I think that the real Catherine was simply in love, or rather in lust, with Culpeper and that it had nothing to do with any grand plan. If her failure to conceive was actually due to Henry's impotence problems then there is no way that she could pass off Culpeper's baby as the King's! Also, what if it was a little Culpeper clone!

Was Catherine Guilty?

This is such a hard question to answer. Catherine's past was colourful but she can hardly be seen as a criminal for her relationship with Francis Dereham. As David Starkey points out, Catherine may have been reckless but neither she or Dereham were married then. It was a sin, but it wasn't a crime punishable by death. She had kept her past a secret and had not corrected the King's view that she was a virgin, but that was all. Was the King honest with her about his past?

Some even question whether she had a full sexual relationship with Thomas Culpeper, as both Catherine and Culpeper confessed to being in love and having secret meetings but denied sex or "carnal knowledge". So, it seems that technically Catherine may not have committed adultery. However, she and Culpeper had committed treason because a new law had been enacted in 1534[29], a law which made it treason for anyone to wish the King harm by words, writing or deed. Catherine Howard, Thomas Culpeper and

Francis Dereham were therefore deemed to have intended to do the King harm by their thoughts and actions. Culpeper had confessed to intending to sleep with the Queen, Dereham's position as the Queen's secretary was seen as an attempt to re-start their romance and Catherine was seen as planning to sleep with both men. Lacey Baldwin Smith explains that Catherine had committed treason because she had betrayed the King as his wife and his subject.[30]

Not only had she betrayed the King, she had impugned the royal issue, the succession, because if she had had a child then the King would never have known if it was his real heir.

Whether or not Catherine had actually slept with Thomas Culpeper, their secret meetings and her love letter to him are evidence of a relationship and it surely would have been consummated at some point. There is only so much handholding and kissing a couple can cope with.

Conclusion

Catherine Howard is a mystery and it is impossible to know what her motives were for having a relationship with Thomas Culpeper and why she put her neck on the line for a few secret liaisons. Popular culture has been cruel to her, although we end up sympathising with her plight. But it is hard to judge a woman we know so little about. The real Catherine Howard could have been a sex-mad girl looking for a good-time or she could have been a victim of manipulation and greed, a toy in the hands of power hungry men. Will we ever know? No, I don't think so.

Notes and Sources

1.   The Six Wives of Henry VIII, Antonia Fraser, p416
2.   Six Wives: The Queens of Henry VIII, David Starkey
3.   Catherine Howard, Lacey Baldwin Smith, p192-194
4.   Ibid., p193
5.   LP xvi. 1426
6.   Starkey

7. Katherine Howard: A Tudor Conspiracy, Joanna Denny, p47
8. Ibid., 157-158
9. Fraser, p386
10. Denny, p86
11. Baldwin Smith, p44
12. Starkey
13. Denny, p239
14. Ibid., p116
15. Starkey
16. Fraser, p391
17. Denny
18. The Chronicle of King Henry VIII of England (The Spanish Chronicle), p82-87
19. Baldwin Smith, p140
20. Starkey
21. Ibid.
22. Ibid.
23. Denny, p165
24. Ibid., p175
25. Baldwin Smith, p170
26. Ibid., p153
27. Denny, p190
28. Suzannah Dunn, p279
29. Baldwin Smith, p175
30. Ibid., p133

Catherine Parr – The Old Nursemaid?

In the final part of our Six Wives' Stereotypes series we look at a wife who I would say has been more ignored and misrepresented than maligned.

When I did a project on Henry VIII and his six wives when I was 11, I thought that Catherine Parr was nothing but a glorified nursemaid, a nurse with a crown and jewels as a perk. I imagined her tending the obese, bad-tempered and ill King, mopping his brow and whispering soothing words of comfort to him. A woman who made his last years more comfortable and who humoured him. And then just last weekend I was watching "The Tudors" and there was Queen Catherine Parr, the nurse, applying a poultice to Henry's leg ulcer. They had made her much younger and more glamorous than my 11 year old imagination, but she was still a nurse!

I also thought of Catherine as an old spinster, for some reason. In my 11 year old mind she was a doddering old lady who Henry picked for her nursing skills!

If people don't associate her name with being Henry's nurse, then they seem to think of her only as the one who survived, the queen who was lucky to outlive the King before he got bored of her and cut off her head!

So, if Catherine Parr has been misrepresented as Henry's nursemaid in his twilight years and the "survivor", who was the real Queen Catherine Parr?

Catherine Parr's Family Background

Catherine was born in 1512, probably in August[1], and was the eldest daughter of Sir Thomas Parr and Maud Green. Her father was descended from Edward III, so Catherine, like Henry VIII's other wives, was descended from King Edward I.

The Parrs had served in the household of John of Gaunt[2] and Catherine's mother, Maud, was one of Queen Catherine of

Aragon's maids-of-honour. Ironically, Catherine was named after Catherine of Aragon!

Catherine Parr's Education

Catherine lost her father when she was just five years old so her mother was responsible for making the decisions regarding Catherine's education. Unlike many girls of her time, Catherine did not just learn needlework, homemaking skills and basic reading and writing, she was given a high standard of education and became fluent in languages such as French, Latin and Italian. Her later love of learning bears testimony to her early education.

The Most Married English Queen

Catherine was far from being 'on the shelf' when Henry VIII took a fancy to her, she had already been married twice before and actually had another suitor planning to marry her.

In 1529, at the age of 17, Catherine Parr married Edward Borough (Burgh), the eldest son of Sir Thomas Borough of Gainsborough Old Hall, Lincolnshire. The marriage was short-lived and childless because Edward died in early 1533. Edward's father, who had just been made Anne Boleyn's Lord Chamberlain, did not take Catherine in but he did provide her with income from three of his manors in Surrey and Kent.[3] It is thought that Catherine went to stay at Sizergh Castle in Cumbria, home of the Dowager Lady Strickland, one of Catherine's father's cousins.

In 1534, Catherine Parr married John Neville, Lord Latimer, of Snape Castle, Yorkshire. It is likely that Lady Strickland and Bishop Tunstall, a friend of Catherine's family, helped to arrange the marriage. It was what Catherine needed, it was a good marriage. Catherine was Latimer's third wife and she became stepmother to his 14 year old son and 9 year old daughter. Latimer died in 1543, probably in the February, leaving Catherine his manor at Stowe, estates around York and silverware. Latimer's will also made Catherine responsible for bringing up Latimer's daughter, Margaret

Neville.[4]

On the 12th July 1543, just 4 months after her husband's burial, Catherine Parr married King Henry VIII in a small ceremony at Hampton Court Palace. However, he had not been Catherine's only suitor in the weeks after Latimer's death, one suitor had to give up on Catherine, making way for the King, and that man had been Thomas Seymour, brother of Jane Seymour. After Henry VIII's death in 1547, Catherine wrote to Seymour telling him that she had wanted to marry him the last time she had been free.[5] It is clear that Seymour's feelings had been requited but along came the King and Catherine was an intelligent woman, she knew she could not deny the King. He offered her and her family wealth, power and security. Catherine had no choice.[6]

King Henry VIII died on the 28th January 1547 and his thrice married widow was finally able to marry the man she loved, Thomas Seymour. The couple courted in secret, sending each other love-letters, and finally married sometime in May 1547. The date of their marriage is not known because it was a secret ceremony. Catherine must have been over the moon. The marriage was a love match and the love letters between them in the lead-up to their marriage clearly show their hopes for the future and their excitement at being reunited.[7] Happiness was to be fleeting though for Catherine, her heart was broken when Seymour started a flirtation, and very inappropriate relationship, with Catherine's ward, the Lady Elizabeth, Henry VIII's teenage daughter. Although the couple were able to patch things up when Elizabeth was sent away in Spring 1548, Catherine Parr died just six days after giving birth to her first child, Mary Seymour. Sadly, even more tragically, there is no record of little Mary after the age of 2. It seems she died as a toddler.

Catherine Parr the Hostage

One little known fact about Catherine Parr is that while she was married to Lord Latimer, she was actually held hostage. It was during the Pilgrimage of Grace of 1536 that the rebels took

Catherine and her stepchildren hostage while they forced Latimer to join their side. Thankfully, Latimer was able to get his wife and children freed and escaped being caught up in the rebellion and its terrible repercussions.

Queen Catherine the Regent

In 1544, Henry VIII appointed Catherine his regent while he went to France. Linda Porter points out that only Catherine of Aragon had performed that role before.[8] Clearly, Henry VIII trusted his sixth wife, one who, like his first wife, was intelligent and capable enough to be left as regent. and who would welcome the responsibility.[9] Porter points out that Catherine obviously had a council to advise and help her, but her three month regency was a success and she deserves credit for it.

Catherine the Mother and Reconciler

Catherine Parr was stepmother to two sets of children: the son and daughter of Lord Latimer and Henry VIII's three children. Not much is known about her relationship with Latimer's son, John Neville. Neville was 14 when she married his father and Linda Porter points out that while Catherine was his stepmother he behaved himself. It was later that the Latimer name was brought into disrepute by allegations of murder and rape. She also kept in touch with him after his father's death and appointed his wife as one of her ladies.[10]

Linda Porter also writes of how close Catherine was to her stepdaughter, Margaret Neville. Not only was Catherine a mother figure, she also encouraged Margaret's love of learning and the young woman's faith. Catherine was devastated by Margaret's death at the young age of twenty-one.[11]

Although Jane Seymour is often credited as reconciling Henry with his daughters, Mary and Elizabeth, it is actually Catherine Parr who deserves the credit. Catherine was able to establish good relationships with all three of Henry's children, even the staunch Catholic, Mary, who held very different religious views to those of her stepmother. Catherine's mother, Maud, had served Mary's mother, Catherine of Aragon, loyally and Catherine and Mary were quite close in age. The two women became close friends and remained so even after the hiccough caused by Catherine's scandalous secret marriage to Thomas Seymour. Although Mary initially disapproved of the marriage, the two women were reconciled and Catherine named her baby girl after her stepdaughter and friend.

Prince Edward was only a few days old when his mother, Jane Seymour, died in October 1537 so Catherine Parr was the only mother he had known. His father's marriage to Anne of Cleves only lasted a few months and he was only 4 years old when Catherine Howard was executed. When his father married Catherine Parr, he was five years old and it was Catherine he called 'Mother'. Linda Porter writes of how his letters to her are proof of her influence and involvement in his education, and she was the link between him and his father, the King. Henry VIII was the rather scary distant father and Catherine was the warm, loving go-between.

As for the precocious Lady Elizabeth, she was completely won over by her stepmother's warmth, charm, wit and intelligence. Elizabeth's love and respect for her stepmother is clearly shown in the beautiful gift given to Catherine by Elizabeth at New Year 1544/1545. The gift was a translation of the famous literary work by Marguerite of Navarre, "Le miroir de l'ame pecheresse", the mirror or glass of the sinful soul. The eleven year old Elizabeth had managed to translate a poem which David Starkey[12] says that today's university students would struggle with. Not only did it show Elizabeth's intelligence, but it also showed her love for her stepmother, in that it would have taken many hours of work. It also showed Elizabeth's appreciation of Catherine's religious views. Starkey wonders if Catherine had actually been sharing Le Miroir with Elizabeth in the summer of 1544 with the mission of converting her. Whatever the truth of the matter, it was a special gift to a beloved stepmother and shows that Catherine was a major influence on the young Elizabeth.

After Henry VIII's death in January 1547, Catherine Parr became Elizabeth's guardian and took her to live with her. Their shared love of religion and learning meant that the two were incredibly close, but in May 1548 Catherine sent Elizabeth to live at her friend Sir Anthony Denny's house and the two never saw each other again. Why? One word: Thomas Seymour.

Thomas Seymour married Catherine Parr sometime in May 1547 and so obviously lived with Catherine and Elizabeth. It was then that he started to act inappropriately with the teenager. He would let himself into her bedroom, sometimes dressed only in a nightshirt, and proceed to kiss, tickle and stroke the girl, even stroking her buttocks. At first, Catherine seems to have put her husband's behaviour down to innocent horseplay and even joined him in Elizabeth's bedroom on occasions. However, things took a rather strange turn when, one day in the garden, Catherine restrained her stepdaughter while Seymour slashed Elizabeth's gown to pieces with his dagger. What was Catherine thinking? We just don't know, but by this time she was pregnant and may have feared losing Seymour. Not a great excuse but in May 1548 Catherine did the right thing and sent Elizabeth away to protect the girl and her reputation and also to protect her own marriage. A very peculiar chain of events!

Although Catherine never saw Elizabeth again, stepmother and stepdaughter did correspond by letter and it is clear that they missed each other. Elizabeth must have been sorely grieved by news of Catherine's death in September 1548.

Although David Starkey is of the view that Catherine's role in re-uniting Henry with his children has been exaggerated, and clearly the King made his own decisions, I do feel that Catherine is partially responsible for Henry's decision to pass the act putting his daughters back into the line of succession. Catherine had welcomed Mary and Elizabeth back to court, had forged close relationships with them and had enabled Henry to become close to them again. Linda Porter describes Catherine as a companion and close friend to Mary and a mother to the young Edward and Elizabeth. Both of their mothers had died when they were young, so she was the only mother that they had ever known. She was there at key stages in their lives and so had a huge impact on them. Catherine also reminded Henry how important his children were in terms of the succession and showed him that he needed to sort out the legalities of this before he died. In 1544, Mary and Elizabeth were restored to the succession and this owed much to Catherine's influence.[13]

Catherine Parr's Faith

Although it is clear that Catherine held Reformist views after her first year of marriage to the King, Linda Porter points out that it is impossible to say what her beliefs were when she married Henry in 1543. Porter says that Catherine is often seen as sacrificing her love for Thomas Seymour and marrying the King so that she could be God's "agent" and do his work, and that it was the opportunity to promote religious change, but we don't know that it was like that at all.[14] Porter explains that although Catherine's family were linked to reform, that it was not obvious or radical enough to worry the King or his conservative councillors, men like Stephen Gardiner.[15] Perhaps Catherine sensibly kept her beliefs to herself, or perhaps she was unsure, at this stage, what she believed. However, in June 1545, Catherine expressed her faith publicly in her book "Prayers Stirring the Mind unto Heavenly Meditations", a compilation of holy works, and seems to have been meeting with Archbishop Thomas Cranmer on an almost daily basis while she was regent. Like Cranmer, Catherine was committed to promoting the idea of worship being in English.

Catherine was also close friends with Catherine Brandon, the Duchess of Suffolk, who, by this time, was an enthusiastic reformer.

Catherine's next book, "Lamentation of a Sinner" was all her own work and was evidence of her views on the dissemination of the Bible, the marriage of the clergy, preaching, death and salvation, and the evils of Rome.[16] Linda Porter comments on how it was definitely evangelical and that some passages showed a Calvinist leaning.[17] It may also have been an attempt by Catherine to heal the divisions in the Church at that time.[18]

The Plot Against Catherine Parr

In 1546, the conservative faction, which included the likes of Stephen Gardiner and Thomas Wriothesley, decided to make a move against the Queen. They used Catherine's reformist beliefs against her and managed to persuade the irritable Henry VIII, who was tiring of his wife's debates with him on religion, to sign a bill of articles against the Queen. However, while Catherine's enemies planned on questioning the queen's ladies and searching the queen's belongings for heretical books, the King spoke of the matter to his physician, Dr Wendy, and the signed bill of articles was 'accidentally' dropped, found by someone and then taken straight to the Queen.[19] How convenient!

Knowing what had happened to Anne Boleyn and Catherine Howard, Catherine understandably became hysterical and Dr Wendy was sent to attend her, the very man the King had spoken to. The physician advised Catherine to submit to the King who would show her mercy.[20] When Henry came rushing to see his ill wife, Catherine submitted to him completely, apologising for displeasing him. The King reassured his distressed wife and left her. The intelligent queen quickly ordered her ladies to get rid of any heretical books they owned and when, the next night, she visited the King and he turned the conversation to matters of religion, asking her opinion, Catherine told Henry:-

"Since thence, therefore, that God hath appointed such a natural difference between man and woman, and your majesty being so excellent in gifts and ornaments of wisdom, and I a silly poor woman, so much inferior in all respects of nature unto you, how then cometh it now to pass that your majesty, in such diffuse causes of religion, will seem to require my judgement which, when I have uttered and said what I can, yet must I, and will I, refer my judgement in this, and in all other cases, to your majesty's wisdom, as my only anchor, supreme head and governor here on earth, next under God to lean unto."

"Not so, by Saint Mary," replied the king, "you are become a doctor, Kate, to instruct us (as we take it) and not to be instructed or directed by us"

Catherine was quick to assure the King that he was mistaken and that she, a lowly woman, would never dare to try and teach her husband:-

"If your majesty take it so," said the queen, "then hath your majesty, very much mistaken, who have ever been of the opinion, to think it very unseemly and preposterous for the woman to take upon her the office of an instructor, or teacher to her lord and husband, but rather to learn of her husband, and to be taught by him, and where I have, with your majesty's leave, heretofore been bold to hold talk with your majesty, wherein sometimes in opinions there hath seemed some difference, I have not done it so much to maintain opinion, as I did it rather to minister talk, not only to end that your majesty might with less grief pass over this painful time of your infirmity, being intentive to our talk, and hoping that your majesty should reap some ease thereby; but also that I, hearing your majesty's learned discourse might receive to myself some profit. thereby."[21]

It was the speech of Catherine's life. The words were those of a humble and submissive wife simply trying to ease her husband's suffering, but they were spoken by an intelligent and pragmatic woman who knew that she had to stroke her husband's ego to survive the plot against her. She said what Henry wanted to hear.

The couple were reconciled and when Wriothesley turned up with armed guards to arrest the Queen, Henry sent him away with a flea in his ear, calling him an "arrant knave, beast and fool."

This story comes from John Foxe, author of Actes and Monuments (Book of Martyrs) and we do not know how much is true, but Linda Porter writes that there were moves against reformers at this time, for example, Anne Askew, who was not as lucky as Catherine. In her biography of Catherine, Elizabeth

Norton wonders if the plot against Catherine was actually a test set by Henry VIII, a test which she passed by submitting to him and taking the chance of mercy offered by her husband.[22] Interesting theory!

Conclusion

As I end this article, I'm left feeling that I have not done this amazing woman justice. Her achievements in my eyes are:-

- Becoming a published author in her own right at a time when women were to be 'seen and not heard'.

- Her influence on the future Elizabeth I – She was a mother and friend to Elizabeth at a time when Elizabeth needed a role model and she helped shape the woman and monarch Elizabeth became. Linda Porter writes of the impact that Catherine had on Elizabeth's education, her faith, her character and her image. Her long and successful reign owed much to her stepmother's influence.[23]

- Survival – Although I get cross with Catherine being labelled as simply the "survivor", she survived everything that Tudor life threw at her: being widowed three times, living with uncertainty, having to give up her true love, becoming queen of England and wife to a man known for his mood swings and the fact that he had executed two wives, acting as regent, going against the grain and causing scandal by marrying Thomas Seymour, and having her heartbroken by the man she loved.

- Her handling of the King – I believe that she made Henry VIII happy in his final years and that she had the intelligence and intuition to know how to handle him.

- Motherhood – Although Catherine died shortly after the birth of her daughter, she was a good mother to five children.

- Being brave enough to follow her heart and marry Thomas

Seymour

I have previously described Catherine as "an attractive and intelligent woman, who combined the intelligence and wit of Anne Boleyn with the prudence and diplomacy of Catherine of Aragon" and I stand by that, but I would also add that she combined the best bits of Henry VIII's previous wives:-

- Catherine of Aragon's diplomacy and loyalty

- Anne Boleyn's wit, charm and intelligence

- Jane Seymour's submissiveness (or knowing when to submit!)

- Anne of Cleves's pragmatism

- Catherine Howard's kindness and warmth

She was an excellent wife queen and I wonder how things would have turned out if Henry had met her many years earlier.

Notes and Sources

1. Katherine the Queen: The Remarkable Life of Katherine Parr, the Last Wife of Henry VII, Linda Porter, p21

2. Ibid., p8

3. Ibid., p57

4. Ibid., p119

5. Ibid., p121

6. Ibid., p139

7. Ibid., p287

8. Ibid., p200

9. Ibid.

10. Ibid., p66

11. Ibid.

12. Elizabeth, David Starkey

13. Last But Not Least – The Enduring Fascination of Katherine Parr, article by Linda Porter

14. Porter, p167

15. Ibid., p167-8

16. Ibid., p241

17. Ibid.

18. Ibid.

19. Ibid., p257

20. Ibid.

21. Book of Martyrs, or, A history of the lives, sufferings and triumphant deaths of the primitive as well as protestant martyrs, John Foxe, p245-249

22. Catherine Parr, Elizabeth Norton, p150

23. Porter, p348

Should Anne Boleyn be Pardoned and Reburied as Queen?

I want to start off this article by explaining how The Anne Boleyn Files website began. In early 2009, I had a very vivid dream about being a spectator at Anne Boleyn's execution. I was a member of the crowd and all I can remember now is hearing Anne's speech, being impressed with her courage and dignity, and being overcome with sheer horror and terror as I realised that this innocent woman was going to be executed. It was one of those times when you are so terrified that you cannot move or speak, you are just rooted to the spot and your mouth is like sandpaper. All I wanted to do was to stop the execution and save Anne. As the French swordsman swung his blade I woke up in a cold sweat and shook Tim awake telling him that he had to design a website for me called The Anne Boleyn Files and that I had to get the real truth out there about Anne Boleyn. That dream led to the birth of The Anne Boleyn Files and I now spend every waking hour researching Anne Boleyn and Tudor history.

Now, I don't believe in reincarnation or the idea that Anne was reaching to me from beyond the grave etc. I think it was just my brain's way of giving me purpose at a time when I really needed it. I was a freelance writer at the time and I've always loved history, so creating The Anne Boleyn Files was the perfect project and it's grown from a project to a full-time job, or perhaps a "mission". My mission statement, if you look on the header of The Anne Boleyn Files website, is to give "The REAL TRUTH about Anne Boleyn "The Most Happy" " and I try to do that by looking at the contemporary sources, researching the period, debunking myths and sharing my findings with you all.

At the end of the day, it is hard to get at the truth when history is written by the victors and attempts were made to obliterate Anne, to pretend that she never existed, or to paint her as a witch and whore, but I try my hardest and I have dedicated my time and energy to revealing the truth as I find it.

Should Anne Boleyn be Pardoned and Reburied as Queen?

So, that's me and my mission but what has that got to do with the question "Should Anne Boleyn be Pardoned and Reburied as Queen"? Well, plenty, because I didn't wake up from that dream with the urgent need to get Anne Boleyn pardoned and reburied. I woke up knowing that my mission was to educate people, and even now, with all I know about Anne and the passion I have for her and her story. I do not feel the need to start a campaign to get her pardoned and to get her re-interred in a magnificent tomb at Westminster Abbey.

Again, I'd just like to re-iterate that I am not criticising anybody who believes that Anne should be pardoned and I have the greatest respect for Wing Commander George Melville-Jackson who, in 2005, called on Charles Clarke, the Home Secretary, to pardon Anne Boleyn and who also wanted her remains laid to rest alongside her daughter, Elizabeth I. The Wing-Commander worked tirelessly on his campaign, writing to the Queen and historians, consulting a barrister etc. but it was all in vain and sadly he died without completing his mission. I wholeheartedly believe that Anne Boleyn was innocent and that her trial was a sham. She suffered a huge miscarriage of justice. I have nothing against those who want to get her pardoned, it's just not my mission and does not fit in with my own feelings on the subject.

So, what are my feelings and why haven't I led a campaign to get Anne Boleyn pardoned and reburied?

- Time and evidence – Anne Boleyn was executed in 1536, nearly five hundred years ago, and, as a barrister told the Wing Commander, it is impossible to go to court and get a judicial review when there is no new evidence. We can see that the indictments against Anne Boleyn and the five men just don't make sense, but a court of her peers accepted these indictments and found her guilty. It is impossible for us now, nearly five hundred years later, to challenge that evidence with our own evidence and we don't even have the full trial records to challenge. We can believe and know in our hearts that Anne Boleyn was innocent, we can question the evidence used against her, we just cannot definitively prove her innocence.

- Where do you stop? – It's not only Anne Boleyn who suffered a miscarriage of justice, what about George Boleyn, Sir Henry Norris, Sir Francis Weston, Sir William Brereton and Mark Smeaton? What about Margaret Pole? What about Francis Dereham? What about all the other innocent victims? I don't feel I could campaign for Anne Boleyn without campaigning for all of them!

- History – As I've said before, history is written by the victors and my mission is to correct bad history and to try and reveal the truth of Anne Boleyn's life and death, not to rewrite history.

- My feelings on Anne Boleyn's resting place – People often say that Anne Boleyn's remains should be dug up and re-interred in somewhere more befitting of a Queen of England and that she is not buried as Queen, however, Anne Boleyn is buried as Queen. In 1876 and 1877 when work was carried out in the Chapel of St Peter ad Vincula, the chapel of the Tower of London, the Victorian workers unearthed the remains of a woman thought to have been Anne Boleyn, in that she was buried where records suggest that Anne was buried. After Dr Mouat had examined the remains of Anne and others found in the chancel, they were "soldered up in thick leaden coffers, and then fastened down with copper screws in boxes made of oak plank, one inch in thickness. Each box bore a leaden escutcheon, on which was engraved the name of the person whose supposed remains were thus enclosed, together with the dates of death, and of the year (1877) of the re-interment."[1] The boxes were then buried where they had been found and memorial tiles placed on the floor of the chancel to mark the graves. These memorial tiles are "octagon panels of white marble, in which are inserted the armorial bearings of those historic persons who were interred in the chancel; their names being inscribed on the border of yellow Siena marble which surrounds each panel."[2] Anne's tile says "Queen Anne Boleyn" so she was buried as a Queen in 1877 and does not rest in some mass grave If you have visited the Chapel of St Peter ad Vincula, you will know that it is a beautiful chapel, a place of God and a place that is used regularly for services. Anne's tile is there for all to see and on the 19th May it receives a basket of roses and flowers from visitors. I, personally, would hate to see the beautiful tiled floor ruined and the peace and tranquillity of the chapel disturbed in order to re-inter Anne in Westminster Abbey. The tile may act as a focal point for Anne Boleyn fans and Tudor history lovers, but Anne Boleyn is not there. Her remains lie under that floor but those who have the same faith that Anne Boleyn had believe that Anne is in Paradise, she is with her Father in Heaven. She has no need to be re-interred and I don't believe for one minute that she is a restless spirit haunting the Tower and other places crying out to be moved to the Abbey. I actually feel that her resting place is a fitting memorial to her. That tile at the Tower of London speaks to people about Anne's story. Tourists wonder why a Queen of England is buried in a little chapel at the Tower and I hope that it makes them ask questions. When I go to visit that tile, I feel such peace and am very moved, I'm not sure I'd feel that in the busy Westminster Abbey.

- Time and Energy – Researching Anne Boleyn's life takes up all of my time, I just do not have the time or energy to launch a campaign, to seek legal advice on the matter and to rally the troops. My aim is to educate and re-educate people about who Anne Boleyn really was and I see that as a hugely important mission.

- It won't change anything – Pardoning Anne Boleyn and moving her body will not, in my opinion, change anything. It won't change history, it won't help Anne and we will still be arguing with those who are convinced that she was a whore and a traitor. I sincerely believe that a pardon will not change people's attitudes, only re-educating people will change those.

Please don't get me wrong, I am passionate about Anne Boleyn – just ask my husband Tim who calls himself an "Anne Boleyn widower" and my children who are completely indoctrinated! – but my passion lies in educating people and challenging the misconceptions that are out there.

Anne Boleyn was Queen of England and mother of Elizabeth I and no-one can take that away from her.

Notes and Sources

1. Notices of the Historic Persons Buried in the Chapel of St Peter ad Vincula in the Tower of London, with an account of the discovery of the supposed remains of Queen Anne Boleyn, by Doyne C Bell, 1877, p30

2. Ibid., p18

The Scandalous and Corrupt Anne Boleyn?

A few weeks ago, I read Alison Weir's new book "Mary Boleyn: The Great and Infamous Whore" (or "Mary Boleyn: Mistress of Kings" to give it its US title), and in it Alison Weir repeats something which she referred to in her earlier book, "The Six Wives of Henry VIII", her idea that Anne Boleyn had been corrupted by her time at the scandalous French court, a court of which Brantôme said "rarely, or never, did any maid or wife leave that court chaste".

Weir writes of Francis I confiding to Anne's uncle, the Duke of Norfolk, that Anne had not lived virtuously there and Anne's husband, Henry VIII, speaking to the Spanish ambassador in 1536 of Anne being 'corrupted' while in France. This is repeated in "Mary Boleyn: The Great and Infamous Whore" when Weir writes of Anne being involved in scandals at the French court and Francis I confiding in Rodolfo Pio about her lack of virtue. Weir goes on to write of how the King confided to the imperial ambassador, Eustace Chapuys, of how he found out about Anne's corruption at the French court after he became sexually involved with her. Later, after Anne's execution, when offered a French bride, Henry comments that he has had "too much experience of French bringing up and manners".

So, according to Alison Weir, a clever Anne Boleyn was able to hide her sexual experience and rather muddied past from Henry VIII and pass herself off as virtuous and Queen material. But what's the evidence for Weir's conclusion? Well, she does give references but they are not all that helpful: "L&P" for the King Francis quote and "S.C." for Chapuys.

Now, L&P, or Letters and Papers, Foreign and Domestic, Henry VIII, has 21 volumes covering 1509 to 1547, and some of them are split into two parts. S.C., or Calendar of State Papers, Spain, has 13 volumes, so it is difficult to find the evidence cited. However, I managed to find the first source that Alison Weir was referring to, the one about Anne Boleyn not living virtuously. These words were actually spoken by Francis I, confiding in Rodolfo Pio, Bishop of Faenza, not the Duke of Norfolk, Faenza then repeats them in a letter to M. Ambrosio on 4th July 1535:-

"Francis also spoke three days ago of the new queen of England, how little virtuously she has always lived and now lives, and how she and her brother and adherents suspect the duke of Norfolk of wishing to make his son King, and marry him to the King's legitimate daughter, though they are near relations." LP viii.985

The Chapuys reference has been more problematic but, with the help of my friend Clare Cherry, I think I've cracked it. Alison Weir says that the King confided in Chapuys in 1536 that Anne Boleyn had been 'corrupted' in France and that a report of these words can be found in the Calendar of State Papers, Spain. Well, I have gone through every document written by Eustace Chapuys in those records in 1536 (L&P, Calendar of State Papers, everything!) and other years and cannot find any reference to Henry VIII saying that Anne had been corrupted in France. I have however found the reference to Henry VIII not wanting to marry a French woman after Anne Boleyn:-

"The King replied that she was too young for him, and that he had had too much experience of French bringing up and manners, alluding to the late concubine, to take her to wife." 'Additions and Corrections', Calendar of State Papers, Spain, Volume 5 Part 2: 1536-1538, Additions and corrections to No.61, 6th June 1536

This was in reference to the idea that Henry VIII should marry "Madame Magdelaine", Madeleine of Valois, Francis I's daughter. I think it is reading far too much into Henry VIII's words to read "bringing up and manners" as referring to sexual experience!

However, Clare thinks, and I agree with her, that Alison Weir is actually basing her theory on Paul Friedmann's interpretation of Henry's words. Friedmann, Anne Boleyn's 19th century biographer, writes:-

"After the death of Anne a courtier told Chapuis (so Chapuis reports) that Henry had refused the hand of the daughter of Francis I [Madeleine of Valois] because she was too young and because in the said concubine he had had too much experience of what the corruption of France was."

Friedmann cites "E.Chapuis to N. de Granvelle, June 6, 1538, Vienna Archives" but this does not exist, it is actually 6th June 1536, the same letter I quote above, mentioning "French bringing up and manners". Not quite corruption, although Friedmann makes the point that it depends on how the original French is read and whether the word used is "nourriture" or "pourriture", "food/fare/nourishment/nurture" or "decay". Henry had either had too much experience of the French bringing up or the French "decay". However you read it, you are reading Friedman's interpretation of Chapuys' interpretation of Henry's words and, in the case of the book "Mary Boleyn", Alison Weir's interpretation of Friedman interpreting Chapuys interpreting Henry!! Aaaggghhh! A bit of a game of Chinese Whispers or Telephone, I feel.

In Letters and Papers, we have the letter that Eustace Chapuys wrote to the Emperor on the 6th June 1536 and the only reference to Anne in that is:-

"He further told me that the bailiff and the other ambassador, his colleague, had proposed the marriage of the eldest daughter of king Francis to this King, but it was lost time altogether, for king Henry would never marry out of his own kingdom. Having then asked him what reason he (Cromwell) had for making such an affirmation, he stated one which, in my opinion, is futile and weak enough, namely, that if he ever marries a foreign princess of great blood and high connexions, should she misbehave herself he could not punish her, and get rid of her, as he had done of his last wife."

Again, it makes no mention of Anne Boleyn's alleged corruption at the French court.

Having looked through the primary sources, I just cannot see the evidence to back up the claim that Anne was corrupted in France and that she was not a virgin when she married Henry VIII. I cannot support such a theory and I will give Anne the benefit of the doubt until I find evidence to the contrary. A virtuous Anne, yes, a corrupt Anne, no.

Notes and Sources

- The Six Wives of Henry VIII by Alison Weir, Chapter 7 "Mistress Anne"

- Mary Boleyn: The Great and Infamous Whore by Alison Weir, p76 (Jonathan Cape UK paperback edition)

- LP viii.985

- Additions and Corrections, Calendar of State Papers, Spain, Volume 5 Part 2: 1536-1538, Additions and corrections to No.61, 6th June 1536

- Anne Boleyn: A Chapter of English history 1527-1536 by Paul Friedmann, p318 in Appendix Note A

- Calendar of State Papers, Spain, Volume 5 Part 2: 1536-1538, no. 61, Eustace Chapuys to Emperor, 6th June 1536

The Sexualization of Anne Boleyn

sexualize, sexualise vb
1.   to make or become sexual or sexually aware
2.   to give or acquire sexual associations

sexualization , sexualisation n

This post has been inspired by a discussion on The History Police Facebook Group regarding the sexualization of historical characters, characters such as Elizabeth Woodville and Anne Boleyn who are often accused of trapping their husbands by using their feminine wiles or sleeping their way to the top, or, in Anne's case, holding out on their lovers until they reach the top.

Now, I don't have a problem with sex (blush, blush), but I do have a problem with the way that Anne Boleyn is often portrayed in novels, movies and the media. When I started The Anne Boleyn Files, I chose to find out the truth about Anne Boleyn, to find the woman behind the myth. The Anne Boleyn I found was not a whore or temptress, but an intelligent, ambitious woman, who had a major impact on those around her and on English history. It angers me that nearly 500 years on she is still being presented as the woman who tempted Henry away from his wife and beloved church, and a woman who even considered incest to keep her man and crown. Even some Anne Boleyn fans are presenting her as some kind of trophy wife, like a modern day footballer's wife or celebrity. Others present her as a tragic heroine, a victim of a husband who sought revenge after being bewitched by her. Sometimes it seems that we haven't moved on from the views of the likes of Chapuys, who called Anne "the Concubine", and the Abbot of Whitby who called her a "common stewed [professional] whore" – nice!

I don't doubt that Anne Boleyn had magnetism and that she enjoyed the courtly love tradition and flirted, but why oh why do some authors and directors have to make it so that her rise to

Queen was based solely on Henry's sexual infatuation with her and her dangling her virginity as bait? It's almost akin to people slurring a woman company director by saying that she only got to that position because she slept with influential people or because she's sexy. Henry VIII was not stupid. I can't see him doing what he did – annulling his first marriage, upsetting his daughter, breaking with the church etc. – just for sex. The Guardian newspaper, in its review of Howard Brenton's "Anne Boleyn" play, spoke of how Anne had Henry VIII in a "sexual stranglehold" and used her sexual power over him to further the cause of religious reform – No, I don't think so, I think there was a bit more to the English Reformation than that.

In a Sunday Times article on "The Other Boleyn Girl" movie, Philippa Gregory describes her story as one of a woman using her sexuality to trap a man and then him seeking revenge. That just makes me want to bang my head against a brick wall. Perhaps I shouldn't let it bother me because it is, at the end of the day, historical fiction, but so many people take "The Other Boleyn Girl" at face value and believe that that's who Anne Boleyn was, a temptress who trapped a King.

In "The Tudors", we see Anne Boleyn holding out on Henry, teasing him and frustrating him by only letting him go so far, and in "The Other Boleyn Girl" we see Henry raping Anne out of frustration. We are led to believe that Anne Boleyn was playing a game, encouraged by her father and uncle. She had learned from her sister's experience as Henry's mistress that the only way she could become queen was to keep Henry interested but to deny him the gift of her "maidenhead". Their whole relationship seems to be based on the promise of passion, the anticipation of that wondrous moment. It is small wonder, therefore, that the marriage is dead within 3 years and that Henry wants rid of Anne.

In these portrayals of Henry and Anne's love story, there is no meeting of minds, no partnership, no shared ambition, just sex or the anticipation of it. How sad. I know that in Henry's love letters to Anne, he talks about wanting to kiss Anne's "pretty dukkys", but the depth of his love for Anne, and not just sexual obsession, is evident from his letters when he is troubled that he may have offended her by asking her to be his one and only mistress. He loves her for who she is and for the fact that he can talk to her as an equal. Here is a woman who tells it like it is, who doesn't just tell him what she thinks he wants to hear, a woman with whom he can debate things and plan the future. That is far more intoxicating to Henry than sex. It is Anne's intelligence and ambition that he is drawn to. It is their shared interests and common goals that bind them together.

Anne Boleyn is not the only victim. Elizabeth Woodville is often portrayed as a woman who used her descent from the mythical Melusine and her knowledge of witchcraft to trap Edward IV and to further her family. Marie Antoinette is depicted as a woman with a voracious appetite for both sexes. Eleanor of Aquitaine was so hot-blooded that she left her frigid husband, Louis VII, for Henry II, and had previously had an affair with her uncle. And what about Jane Boleyn, Lady Rochford? She is unfairly portrayed as someone who betrayed her husband and sister-in-law because of her jealousy of their close, or even incestuous, relationship, and as the woman who acted as agent provocateur to Catherine Howard and Thomas Culpeper, taking a sexual thrill out of their secret meetings and enjoying being a voyeur. Oh, and of course Elizabeth I became one of the greatest English monarchs because she was the Virgin Queen and used her sexuality, and the magnetism that she had inherited from her mother, to get what she wanted. Yes, Elizabeth used her single status and the marriage market for diplomacy, but the success of her reign did not rest solely on her sexuality and her status as the "Virgin Queen", she actually had a brain too.

Alexandra, a member of the History Police Facebook group, summed up my feelings on this issue well when she commented on Boudicca, saying, "I think Boudicca was sexy because she was powerful, not powerful because she was sexy" . We are doing historical characters a grave injustice when we credit their success and power to sex and their sex appeal.

Right, I think I'll get off my soapbox now!

Notes and Sources

- Collins English Dictionary Complete and Unabridged, Harper Collins 1991, 1994, 1998, 2000, 2003
- The History Police Facebook Group
- The Guardian Review of the play "Anne Boleyn" by Howard Brenton, Michael Billington, 29 July 2010
- "Philippa Gregory watches as her bestseller 'The Other Boleyn Girl' gets the Hollywood treatment", The Times and Sunday Times, February 15, 2008

Anne Boleyn – "The Great Whore"

The idea that Anne Boleyn was a whore or strumpet has absolutely nothing to do with her own moral standards. It stems from public opinion of her, the opinions voiced by Catherine of Aragon's supporters and those who set out to blacken her name after her execution and during Mary I's reign.

Both the public and Catherine of Aragon's supporters blamed Anne Boleyn for stealing the King away from Catherine, usurping Catherine's place as Queen, turning Henry against the Catholic Church and for causing the tyrannical behaviour of the King which resulted in good men (Sir Thomas More and Bishop John Fisher) losing their lives and monasteries being ransacked. Phew! No wonder Anne Boleyn was so unpopular when she first became Queen!

Names for Anne

It was believed that for her to hold this kind of power and influence over the King (to make him act this way), Anne must have some kind of sexual hold over him, after all, in those days sexuality was a woman's only power! So, Anne became known as:-

- "The Great Whore"
- "The King's Whore" and a "naughty paike"
- "The concubine", "the she-devil" and "the whore" – Chapuys, the Imperial Ambassador
- "The Goggle Eyed Whore" – Margaret Chanseler
- "Common stewed [professional] whore" – the Abbot of Whitby
- "The scandal of Christendom" – Catherine of Aragon

When we look at Anne through the eyes of the public who loved (and were still loyal to) Catherine of Aragon and who saw their beloved King Henry turn into a man who now committed brutal and atrocious acts on a seemingly daily basis, we can well understand why they thought of her as an evil woman who had some kind of hold over the once virtuous King.

The injustice of it all!

But to think of Anne Boleyn as some kind of harlot or sexual predator who stole the King's heart from the true queen is to do her a mighty injustice.

There is absolutely no evidence at all that Anne was sexually immoral, that she had sexual relationships before her relationship with Henry VIII or that she was unfaithful to him. Anne is thought to have held on to her virginity until shortly before her marriage to the King and it was the King who "deflowered" her.

What we do have is evidence that Anne Boleyn was a religious and virtuous woman, who was charitable and giving (she gave alms regularly and sewed garments for the poor), and a woman who spoke out against injustice – she argued with Thomas Cromwell over the fact that money taken from the monasteries was going into royal coffers rather than to the poor and needy.

By the time of her execution, she had actually become quite popular and Sir William Kingston, her jailer, was worried that the Tower of London would be stormed by her supporters. The public was shocked by her treatment and disapproved of the King's behaviour with Jane Seymour.

It was unfair of people like Eustace Chapuys to blame Anne for breaking up the marriage of the King and Catherine of Aragon. Chapuys never properly acknowledged Anne as Queen and always referred to her as "the concubine" or "whore" in his dispatches because he felt that Catherine was the true Queen. However, the marriage of Henry VIII and Catherine of Aragon was over years before Anne even came on the scene. Kelly Hart in "The Mistresses of Henry VIII" writes that the first rumours of annulment of the marriage started to circulate in 1514 and Retha Warnicke ("The Rise and Fall of Anne Boleyn") writes of how the King had decided to annul the marriage before even considering a new wife.

Now I know that I have been accused of being biased about Anne (and I am really!), but I certainly don't believe that she was a martyr or a perfect woman. I cannot condone her behaviour with a still married man but I feel that it is unjust to paint her as a harlot, witch or adulteress. Henry VIII was responsible for his actions. I know that Anne had some influence over him and that he discussed things with her, but she cannot take all the blame for the atrocities he committed or for the man that he turned out to be. The change from virtuous prince to tyrannical monster was not all down to Anne.

Anne Boleyn's Remains –
The Exhumation of Anne Boleyn

I decided to write this article because there is so much false information out there about the restoration work at St Peter ad Vincula Chapel in the 19th century, the exhumation of Anne Boleyn and various other Tudor remains, and Anne Boleyn's resting place.

I recently purchased a copy of the 1877 "Notices of the Historic Persons Buried in the Chapel of St Peter ad Vincula in the Tower of London, With an Account of the Discovery of the Supposed Remains of Anne Boleyn" by Doyne C Bell (Secretary to Her Majesty's Privy Purse). This book is a full record of the restorations in 1876 and 1877, including the findings of Dr Frederick J Mouat (professor of medicine) who examined the remains found, so I can tell you exactly what was found in the 19th century and what was done with it.

The Restorations

In his "History of England", Lord Macaulay said of St Peter ad Vincula:-

"I cannot refrain from expressing my disgust at the barbarous stupidity which has transformed this interesting little church into the likeness of a meeting house in a manufacturing town. In truth there is no sadder spot on earth than this little cemetery. Death is there associated not, as in Westminster and St Paul's, with genius and virtue, with public veneration and with imperishable renown; not as in our humblest churches and churchyards, with everything that is most endearing in social and domestic charities: but with what ever is darkest in human nature and in human destiny; with the savage triumph of implacable enemies, with the inconstancy, the ingratitude, the cowardice of friends, with all the miseries of fallen greatness and of blighted fame.

"Thither have been carried through successive ages, by the rude hands of gaolers, without one mourner following, the bleeding relics of men, who had been captains of armies, the leaders of parties, the oracles of senates, and the ornaments of courts."[1]

And it was the unsightly state of the chapel, along with the need to do repairs for sanitary reasons, which led to Sir Charles Yorke, Constable of the Tower, to submit plans for restoration to Queen Victoria in 1876. The resulting decision was that "the chapel should be, as far as possible, architecturally restored to its original condition, and also suitably arranged as a place of worship for the use of the residents and garrison of the Tower."[2]

The proposed restoration work included relaying the pavement, which had sunk over the years, and to install some kind of heating. It was when the pews were removed and the pavement stones lifted in August 1876, that "the resting places of those who had been buried within the walls of the chapel... had been repeatedly and it was feared almost universally desecrated."[3] Due to the fact that the ground needed to be cleared so that proper foundations could be laid for the pavement, it was necessary to remove the remains to the crypt, unless they were in stable vaults. The remains were therefore "carefully collected and enclosed in boxes, with suitable inscriptions; and all the coffins which were found intact were at once removed to the crypt."[4]

The Restoration of the Chancel

In October 1876 the issue of the chancel came to the forefront. Records showed that the Tudor queens Anne Boleyn and Catherine Howard were buried there, along with the Dukes of Somerset, Northumberland and Monmouth, so it had been decided to leave the chancel undisturbed and to just lay the new pavement over the top of the old. However, the Surveyor examined the area and found that the pavement had sunk in two places and there was no other option but to remove it and to replace it with tiles or symmetrical paving so that it would be in keeping with the rest of the chapel.

Doyne C Bell used historical sources to create a plan of the resting places of the queens and dukes and it was decided that any remains found should be re-interred on the same spot and labelled.

The remains of Anne Boleyn

When the pavement was lifted in the area thought to have been the resting place of Anne Boleyn, the bones of a female were found at a depth of about two feet, "not lying in the original order, but which had evidently for some reason or other been heaped together into a smaller space."[5] The bones were then examined by Dr Mouat who confirmed that they belonged to "a female of between twenty-five and thirty years of age, of a delicate frame of body, and who had been of slender and perfect proportions; the forehead and lower jaw were small and especially well formed. The vertebrae were particularly small, especially one joint (the atlas), which was that next to the skull, and they bore witness to the Queen's 'lyttel neck.'"[6] Although the bones were mixed up, there were no further female remains at that spot. The bones of George Boleyn were not found but it was thought that the ground had been disturbed in the late 18th century and his remains removed then, or that he was buried further towards the north wall, in an area not touched by the restoration work.

Dr Mouat's Findings

Of the remains of Anne Boleyn, Dr Mouat wrote in a memorandum:-

"The bones found in the place where Queen Anne Boleyn is said to have been buried are certainly those of a female in the prime of life, all perfectly consolidated and symmetrical, and belong to the same person.

"The bones of the head indicate a well-formed round skull, with an intellectual forehead, straight orbital ridge, large eyes, oval face and rather square full chin. The remains of the vertebrae, and the bones of the lower limbs, indicate a well-formed woman of middle height, with a short and slender neck. The ribs show depth and roundness of chest. The hands and feet bones indicate delicate and well-shaped hands and feet, with tapering fingers and a narrow foot."[7]

He went on to say that they were consistent with descriptions of Anne and the sitter of the Holbein painting owned by the Earl of Warwick.

Dr Mouat also wrote a detailed report of his examination of the skeleton, in which he noted that Anne was about 5' – 5'3 inches in height. A careful examination of the finger bones did not show any evidence of a sixth finger or any type of malformation.

Other Remains

Some male bones were found close to the remains of Anne Boleyn. These were examined and found to have belonged to a tall man of around the age of 50. It was thought that they belonged to Protector Somerset (Edward Seymour) who was recorded as being laid to rest between Anne Boleyn and Catherine Howard in 1551. The bones of another man of about 50 years of age were then found. These were identified as the Duke of Northumberland, executed in 1553, who was also laid to rest between the queens.

Nearer to the wall of the chancel, in a south-east direction, the bones of two females were found. The first set belonging to a female of 30-40 years of age and the other to an elderly female. The team identified these as belonging to Lady Rochford and Margaret Pole, Countess of Salisbury.

Beneath a stone bearing the name of Sir Allan Apsley, Lieutenant of the Tower, who died in 1630, the bones of a man were found. Then the leg bones of a tall man, identified as the Duke of Monmouth, were found in the expected place, as recorded "under the communion table". Another large skeleton was found under the Duke of Monmouth's remains, but these could not be identified.

The remains of Catherine Howard were not found and it was thought that this was due to her youth (young bones are softer and more cartilaginous and so disintegrate more rapidly) and the use of lime in her interment - lime was found in the place thought to have been her grave.

The Duke of Northumberland's Remains

Dr Mouat recorded that "these bones evidently belonged to a large man, about six feet in height; and aged about 50 years."[8]

Margaret Pole's Remains

Dr Mouat recorded that these bones belonged to "a tall and aged female".[9]

Lady Rochford's Remains

The only notes that were made regarding the remains of Jane Boleyn, Lady Rochford, were that they belonged to a woman of around 40 and were found where expected, next to the supposed grave of Catherine Howard. Lady Rochford was executed on the same day as Catherine. in February 1542

What Happened to the Remains?

The records of the meeting held on the 13th April 1877 in the Chapel of St Peter ad Vincula, made by Bell, tell us that the remains of the seven people found in the chancel in November 1876 were:-

"soldered up in thick leaden coffers, and then fastened down with copper screws in boxes made of oak plank, one inch in thickness. Each box bore a leaden escutcheon, on which was engraved the name of the person whose supposed remains were thus enclosed, together with the dates of death, and of the year (1877) of the re-interment.

"They were then placed in the respective positions in the chancel in which the remains had been found, and the ground having been opened, they were all buried about four inches below the surface, the earth was then filled in, and concrete immediately spread over them."[10]

They were put back in the positions recorded by Bell and were buried with respect.

A memorial tablet of those buried in the chapel was also produced and placed on the wall near the entrance door, where it can still be seem today. It reads:-

List of Remarkable Persons Buried in this Chapel

Gerald Fitzgerald, Earl of Kildare 1534

John Fisher, Bishop of Rochester 1535

Sir Thomas More 1535

George Boleyn, Viscount Rochford 1536

Queen Anne Boleyn 1536

Thomas Cromwell, Earl of Essex 1540

Margaret of Clarence, Countess of Salisbury 1541

Queen Katharine Howard 1542

Jane, Viscountess Rochford 1542

Thomas, Lord Seymour of Sudeley 1549

Edward Seymour, Duke of Somerset 1551

Sir Ralph Vane 1552

Sir Thomas Arundell 1552

John Dudley, Duke of Northumberland 1553

Lord Guildford Dudley 1554

Lady Jane Grey 1554

Henry Grey, Duke of Suffolk 1554

Thomas Howard, Duke of Norfolk 1572

Sir John Perrott 1592

Philip, Earl of Arundel 1595

Robert Devereux, Earl of Essex 1601

Sir Thomas Overbury 1613

Thomas, Lord Grey of Wilton 1614

Sir John Eliot 1632

William, Viscount Stafford 1680

Arthur, Earl of Essex 1683

James, Duke of Monmouth 1685

George, Lord Jeffreys 1689
John Rotier 1703
Edward, Lord Griffin 1710
William, Marquis of Tullibardine 1746
William, Earl of Kilmarnock 1746
Arthur, Lord Balmerino 1746
Simon, Lord Fraser of Lovat 1747

Bell's book then goes on to give an account of the arrest, imprisonment, death and burial of each person on this list.

The Scaffold Memorial

In 1866, Queen Victoria commanded that the spot where it was thought that Queen Anne Boleyn and others had been executed should be cordoned off by a railing and a memorial plaque placed there. A brass plate on a stone was inscribed with the following words:-

> "Site of the ancient scaffold: on this spot Queen Anne Boleyn was beheaded on the 19th May, 1536."

Today we have the modern glass memorial which was unveiled in 2006. It was designed by Brian Catling and features two engraved circles with a glass-sculpted pillow at the centre and a beautiful poem etched around the sides.

Notes and Sources

1. Macaulay's History of England, Vol. I, pp 628-9, quoted in Notices of the Historic Persons Buried in the Chapel of St Peter ad Vincula in the Tower of London, With an Account of the Discovery of the Supposed Remains of Anne Boleyn" by Doyne C Bell 1877, p8-9

2. Bell, p10

3. Ibid., p15

4. Ibid., p16

5. Ibid., p20

6. Ibid., p21

7. Ibid., p26

8. Ibid., p29

9. Ibid.

10. Ibid., p30

Anne Boleyn's Body Found?

In my previous article, "Anne Boleyn's Remains – The Exhumation of Anne Boleyn", I wrote about the restoration of St Peter ad Vincula Chapel in 1876 and the exhumation of the bodies in the chancel, including that of Anne Boleyn. But did the skeleton found actually belong to Anne Boleyn? Alison Weir[1] thinks not.

No, it's not Anne Boleyn

In her book, "The Lady in the Tower", Alison Weir discusses the findings of the Victorians and the records of Dr Mouat, the doctor who examined the remains found in November 1876. She argues that the Victorians made a mistake. Dr Mouat[2] gave the skeleton's age as between 25 and 30 years of age and described the woman as having a "square, full chin". Alison Weir points out that not only does this description not tally with the widely accepted birthdate of 1501 (and therefore an age of 35), it also does not match Anne Boleyn's appearance. Weir concludes that the bones of a petite female with a square jaw must surely be those of Catherine Howard, who Holbein shows with a square jaw, rather than anne Boleyn.[3]

Weir goes on to look at the descriptions of another skeleton found in the place where Catherine Howard and Lady Rochford were thought to have been buried. Dr Mouat recorded that these bones belonged to a female of "rather delicate proportions" and "about thirty to forty years of age" and identifies them as belonging to Jane Boleyn, Lady Rochford. Weir concludes that these bones are more likely to belong to the 35 year old Anne Boleyn, rather than Lady Rochford who was probably born around 1512,. She believes that Anne's memorial stone actually marks the resting place of Lady Rochford, not Anne.[4]

Yes, it is Anne Boleyn

Doyne C Bell, author of 1877 "Notices of the Historic Persons Buried in the Chapel of St Peter ad Vincula in the Tower of London, With an Account of the Discovery of the Supposed Remains of Anne Boleyn", Secretary to Her Majesty's Privy Purse and member of the committee undertaking the restorations of the chapel, drew up his plan of the resting places of Anne Boleyn and others in the chancel based on "consulting various historical authorities". The fact that this body was found exactly where Bell's plan showed Anne Boleyn to be buried and "no other female bones were found on this spot"[5] makes me think that they do belong to Anne. The bones belonging to a 35-40 year old female were found in the grave where Catherine Howard and Lady Rochford were said to have been buried, so couldn't that body be that of Lady Rochford?

Obviously if you believe that Anne was born in 1507, then Dr Mouat's description of the skeleton belonging to a 25-30 year old woman makes sense as Anne would have been 28/29 when she was executed. If you believe in a 1501 birthdate then Anne was 34/35 when she was executed so it's slightly out, but then the Victorians did not have access to the same technology that we have today. The description doesn't exactly fit Catherine Howard either, seeing as she was 17-21 years of age when she died (depending on which birthdate you believe in). One feature of the skeleton that really does make me think of Anne Boleyn is the description of the hands:-

"delicate and well-shaped hands and feet, with tapering fingers and a narrow foot."[6]

We know that Elizabeth I was proud of her long, elegant fingers and I am convinced that she inherited these from her mother, Anne Boleyn.

As far as the argument over the "square, full chin is concerned"[7], it depends on which portrait of Anne Boleyn you believe to be most accurate. The "Anne Boleyn after Holbein" portrait (from Hever Castle) shows Anne with a squarish chin, as do the Holbein sketches. I personally believe that the Hever rose and NPG portraits are closest to what Anne Boleyn looked like and although they show her with a pointed chin, Dr Mouat's description described the face as being oval and perhaps the portrait lengthened Anne's chin slightly – who knows? It is hard to know exactly how square and full Dr Mouat meant and we obviously don't know for sure exactly what Catherine Howard or Lady Rochford looked like.

Also, if Lady Rochford was "born in 1512 at the latest"[8] and was executed in 1542, then she would have been aged at least 30 when she died, probably older as that would have made her only 12 in 1524 when she got married. Julia Fox,[9] Jane Boleyn's biographer puts Jane's year of birth at 1505, which would make Jane 37 years old when she died, so it makes sense that the bones of a 35-40 year old, found in the grave where she and Catherine Howard were recorded to have been buried, did indeed belong to Jane Boleyn, Lady Rochford.

My conclusion is that there is no reason to think that the Victorians were wrong in their identification of Anne Boleyn's remains. I know that their identification relied on circumstantial evidence, the fact that the body lay where they expected to find Anne Boleyn, but there is no hard evidence to suggest that it wasn't Anne. Whatever the real truth of the matter, Anne Boleyn was buried in the chancel, next to her beloved brother, George, so even if she's not directly under that tile, she is not far away. John Bayley, the 19th century author of "The History and Antiquities of the Tower of London" writes:-

"In front of the altar, repose the beauteous Anna Boleyn, and the guilty Catherine Howard, two ill-fated wives of Henry VIII: the former suffered in 1536, under charge of adultery not clearly proved; and the latter, upon full conviction of the same crime, in 1541. Here also sleeps the headless body of George lord Rochford, the innocent brother of the former. Involved in her accusation, he preceded, by two days, his unfortunate sister to the grave, as his infamous wife, a principal instrument in their death, accompanied, unpitied, her mistress, Catherine Howard, in execution and in sepulture."[10]

I have seen it written online that Anne Boleyn's bones were identified as Anne because they were mixed up with pieces of the elm chest that she was buried in, but this is not true. The records from 1876 make no mention of any pieces of elm wood being found with the bones and I am not sure that you'd expect to find any remains of a wooden box 340 years on.

Alison Weir[11] writes of how Yeoman Warder, Geoffrey Abbot, who has written several books on the Tower, suggests, from the information of an uncited Tudor source, that actually George and Anne Boleyn were buried at opposite ends of the vault and that Lady Rochford was buried next to her husband. Agnes Strickland writes of how Anne "was thrust into a grave that had been prepared for her by the side of her murdered brother".[12] Hmm...

Other Possible Burial Sites

There are a few legends regarding the resting place of Anne Boleyn, with some people believing that her body is not in the Tower of London at all:-

- Salle Church, Norfolk – Agnes Strickland writes of the "curious tradition" from Anne Boleyn's "native Norfolk" which tells of how Anne's remains were secretly removed from the Tower of London at night, taken to Salle Church, "the ancient burial place of the Boleyns, and there interred at midnight, with the holy rites that were denied to her by her royal husband" under an unmarked slab of black marble. Although Strickland states that there is no evidence to support this legend, she does quote Sir Thomas Wyatt: "God provided for her corpse sacred burial, even in a place as it were consecrate to innocence" , saying that this could suggest that Wyatt was in on the secret and had something to do with the removal of Anne's remains. In her book "Anne Boleyn",[13] Norah Lofts writes of how she visited Salle Church and was shown the black marble slab by the sexton. She asked if it had ever been lifted and was told that the patron of the church was not in favour of having it lifted for investigation. The sexton also told her that Anne was said to "walk" the church every year on the night of the anniversary of her execution and that one year on the 19th May he had been keeping vigil when "a great hare" appeared in the church and led him "a fine chase". Lofts explained to the man that a hare was one of the forms that a witch was supposed to be able to turn into at will and that Anne was supposed to have been a witch. What nonsense! Alison Weir writes of how the Salle Church myth was debunked when the slab at the church was lifted and nothing was found underneath it[14] but an article entitled "Where was Anne Boleyn Buried?"[15] on the Reepham Benefice website (the benefice of Salle Church) makes no mention of the slab ever being lifted.

- Horndon-on-the-Hill, Essex – Agnes Strickland also tells of this legend, saying that "in the ancient church of Horndon-on-the-Hill in Essex, a nameless black marble monument is also pointed out by village antiquaries as the veritable monument of this queen."[16] Strickland thinks that this legend and the Salle Church legend grew out of "rumours of the murdered queen's removal from the Tower chapel" which "were at one time in circulation among the tenants and dependants of her paternal house, and were by them orally transmitted to their descendants as matter of fact."

- St Mary's Church, Erwarton, Suffolk – According to legend, Henry VIII and Anne Boleyn often stayed at Erwarton Hall in Suffolk and Anne loved the place so much that she gave instructions that her heart should be buried in the local church. During renovations at the local St Mary's Church in 1838, a heart-shaped casket was found set into an alcove in the north aisle and legend has it that Sir Philip Parker of Erwarton Hall, Anne's uncle, was the one who buried Anne's heart there. The casket was then reburied beneath the organ and a plaque states that Anne Boleyn's heart is buried there.[17] Alison Weir writes of how this legend is unlikely because heart burial was only fashionable until the end of the 14th century (yet it is said that Henry VIII buried Jane Seymour's heart in the Chapel Royal at Hampton Court Palace), and the uncle's name is wrong. Anne's aunt, Amata Boleyn was married to Sir Philip Calthorpe. Whatever the truth of the matter, the village pub is called "The Queen's Head"!

A Mass Grave

Many people are under the impression that all of the remains found during the Victorian restorations were buried together in a mass grave. This is not true.

The seven sets of bones found in the chancel were identified and re-interred in separate, labelled boxes under the chancel floor and given memorial tiles. The remains found in the main part of the church, of which there were many, were collected, taken to the crypt "and enclosed in boxes, with suitable descriptions."

Queen Victoria was saddened by the findings of the restoration team, who found that coffins had been deliberately broken up in the past to make room for new "occupants", and only gave her blessing to the restoration plans "with the express condition that the greatest care and reverence should be exercised in this removal, and that a careful record should be kept of every sign of possible identification which might come to light."[18] The Victorians did their best to treat the remains with respect, though of course they did not raise the whole floor.

Notes and Sources

1. The Lady in the Tower, Alison Weir

2. The findings of Dr Frederick Mouat published in "Notices of the Historic Persons Buried in the Chapel of St Peter ad Vincula in the Tower of London, With an Account of the Discovery of the Supposed Remains of Anne Boleyn" by Doyne C Bell, 1877

3. Alison Weir, p326

4. Ibid., p327

5. Doyne C Bell, p21

6. Dr Mouat in Bell, p26

7. Ibid.

8. Weir, p326

9. Jane Boleyn: The True Story of the Infamous Lady Rochford, Julia Fox, p8

10. The History and Antiquities of the Tower of London, John Bayley, 1821, p120

11. Weir, p324

12. Lives of the Queens of England: From the Norman Conquest – Volume 2, Agnes Strickland, p700

13. Anne Boleyn, Norah Lofts, p183-185

14. Weir, p323

15. Where was Anne Boleyn Buried?, Reepham Benefice Website

16. Strickland, p701

17. The St Mary's Church, Erwarton website

18. Bell, p16

Should Henry VIII be Exhumed and Would it Provide the Answer to his Tyranny?

On Sunday 13th February 2011, there was a report on The Daily Express and Sunday Express website entitled "Queen Asked: May We Dig Up Henry VIII?". The article opened by informing readers that the Queen had been asked for permission to exhume Henry VIII's body to investigate claims that a rare disease had caused his tyrannical behaviour.

American researchers Catrina Whitley and Kyra Kramer believe that Henry had "Kell-positive" blood, and suffered from the related genetic disease McLeod's syndrome. Dr Whitley, a bioarchaeologist, said that mental illness could explain why Henry went from virtuous prince to tyrant and could clear his name.

Was Henry VIII Kell Positive?

Now, this request for permission to exhume Henry VIII's body is based on a new theory published in an article in "The Historical Journal" entitled "A New Explanation for the Reproductive Woes and Midlife Decline of Henry VIII" by Catrina Banks Whitley and Kyra Kramer. As the Daily Express says, Whitley and Kramer believe that Henry VIII was positive for the Kell blood group and that this was responsible for the miscarriages and infant deaths experienced by Catherine of Aragon and Anne Boleyn. This also, allegedly, caused him to suffer with the related genetic disorder, McLeod Syndrome, which they think could have caused physical and mental impairment. I have read Whitley and Kramer's full article and here are the key points they make:-

- That Catherine of Aragon and Anne Boleyn had many miscarriages.

- That his changing policies and personality, which are noticeable as he reached middle age, supports David Starkey's observation that there were two very different Henry's - the one of his youth and the one of his old age.

- That Henry VIII had Kell blood group and McLeod syndrome.

- That a Kell positive male could cause his partner to suffer miscarriages/stillbirths after the first pregnancy.

- That McLeod Syndrome, which typically begins between the ages of 30 and 40, had the following symptoms: cardiomyopathy, muscular myopathy, psychiatric abnormality, and motor neuropathy, and that Henry VIII exhibited most of those symptoms

- That fertility was obviously not an issue in Henry's case, seeing as his partners had had a total of 11-13 pregnancies. The problem was foetal death - miscarriages and stillbirths.

- That a Kell positive father creates reproductive problems just like the problems caused by a Rhesus incompatible pregnancy.

- That when a Kell negative mother becomes pregnant by a Kell positive man, each pregnancy has a 50/50 chance of being Kell positive, and that the first pregnancy is usually carried to term and results in a healthy baby. However, subsequent pregnancies are at risk.

- That the Kell positive gene can be traced back to Jacquetta of Luxembourg, mother of Elizabeth Woodville and Henry VIII's great-grandmother.

- That McLeod Syndrome begins to manifest between the ages of 30 and 40 and that as well as muscle weakness and nerve deterioration, symptoms include paranoia, depression, personality alterations and schizophrenic type behaviour which worsen over time.

- That Henry VIII's paranoia and the way he began to get

rid of people who he saw as challenges to his throne can be explained by McLeod Syndrome.

- That the rise and fall of Anne Boleyn and his treatment of Cromwell, Margaret Pole and religious reformers show Henry's paranoia and symptoms of McLeod's syndrome.

Now, while this is all very interesting, I can't say that I believe this theory at all, it just hasn't convinced me. I'm not a medical expert, but when I Googled McLeod Syndrome, I found that symptoms included tics, tongue biting, irregular limb contractions, seizures, behaviour changes and late-onset dementia. Well, I'm not aware of Henry VIII having seizures or tics. The article I found also suggested that it usually manifests around the age of 50 and is slowly progressive. Henry VIII was in his 40s in the 1530s when it is said that his behaviour became more tyrannical.

As far as Henry being Kell positive is concerned, I did find that when a Kell negative woman is pregnant by a Kell positive father maternal antibodies can be transferred across the placenta and can cause severe anaemia and serious complications, but I'm not sure that there is enough evidence to conclude that Henry VIII was Kell positive. I guess this is why the Queen is being asked for permission to exhume his body.

Does it Explain his 'Reproductive Woes'?

The whole theory depends on what we believe about the obstetric history of Henry VIII's wives and mistresses. According to Sir John Dewhurst, there is only evidence for Catherine of Aragon having six pregnancies and although this is quite a large number her first child was stillborn whereas her second child lived for 52 days and her fifth pregnancy resulted in Princess Mary. In my opinion that really doesn't tie in with Henry VIII being Kell positive. Dewhurst goes on to say that there is only evidence to support Anne having two pregnancies (Eric Ives says three), the first resulting in a healthy baby girl, Elizabeth, and the second a miscarriage. I'm just not sure that we can say that Henry VIII had "reproductive woes" when we also consider that he had a healthy son by Bessie Blount, a possible two children by Mary Boleyn and a healthy son by Jane Seymour. We don't have enough data to conclude that Henry was Kell positive and I don't think that Catherine's obstetric history was at all unusual in a time of poor hygiene and a lack of knowledge concerning ante-natal care. Even today, we all know women who have suffered miscarriages or still-births for no apparent reason, these tragedies are a sad fact of life.

Henry VIII's Tyranny

As far as McLeod Syndrome is concerned, I'm more inclined to believe that Henry's paranoia, mood swings and tyranny were due to a combination of factors:-

- Pain – Living with constant pain, as Henry was, is bound to make you grumpy, impatient and irrational. I know a simple headache can cause me to lash out at my husband!

- Frustration – Henry's leg ulcers made it impossible for him to enjoy activities like tennis and jousting, and that must have been so frustrating for the sport-loving king. He also must have been embarrassed by the smell from his leg and the way that he had to depend on others.

- Challenges to his authority – Monarchs had to deal with challenges to their authority quickly and brutally, that was the way of the world and the way to keep your throne. Others had to be deterred from rebelling or challenging him.

- Head injuries – Henry VIII had two jousting accidents, both of which involved him hitting his head, and he suffered headaches as a result of these accidents. The second accident resulted in the King being unconscious for two hours so Henry may well have suffered an injury to his brain in this accident. When I wrote about Henry's jousting accident recently, many people commented on how they had known friends and relatives to undergo complete personality changes after suffering a head injury so this may well be a factor in

Henry's worsening behaviour and mood swings.

- Henry's personality – Historian J.J.Scarisbrick makes the point that Henry was no more cruel after his 1536 jousting accident than before, and I think that Henry always had cruelty in his character. We may look on his reign and think that his behaviour got worse but is it simply because he was dealing with more threats and problems?

It is so hard to know, isn't it? We all have our own theories about Henry VIII's psyche and behaviour. So, should we exhume his body and take hair and bone samples to find out if Henry did suffer from a genetic disorder?

No.

That is just my opinion but I believe it for the following reasons:-

- I don't want to see a mess being made of St George's Chapel, a place of worship.

- It sets a dangerous precedent and we'll have ancient tombs being unearthed all over the place.

- It strikes me as disrespectful in that we would be doing it simply to satisfy our own morbid curiosity, it does not benefit us in any way.

If renovation work was being carried out on the Chapel then I might feel differently, but it's not.

Notes and Sources

- Queen Asked: May We Dig Up Henry?, article from Express. co.uk, Sunday 13th February 2011

- "A New Explanation for the Reproductive Woes and Midlife Decline of Henry VIII" by Catrina Banks Whitley and Kyra Kramer, The Historical Journal, 53, 4 (2010), pp. 827–848, Cambridge University Press 2010

- "The Alleged Miscarriages of Catherine of Aragon and Anne Boleyn", article by Sir John Dewhurst

- Wikipedia page on Kell Antigen System
- Wikipedia page on Hemolytic Disease of the Newborn (anti-Kell)
- Wikipedia page on McLeod Syndrome

Anne Boleyn and
Catherine of Aragon – Part 1

Anne Boleyn is often blamed for the ill treatment suffered by Catherine of Aragon and her daughter Mary. Some even go as far as accusing her of poisoning Catherine to death.

Now, whilst most of us agree that Anne Boleyn was no saint (well, according to John Foxe she was a saint!), was she really guilty of the awful treatment that these people had at the hands of the King?

Before I consider Anne's supposed ill treatment of Catherine, I think we first need to look at Catherine's feelings and behaviour towards the King and Anne Boleyn.

You can't help but feel sorry for this woman who was Henry's wife for nearly 24 years and who never stopped believing that she was Henry's one and only true wife.

Catherine of Aragon was a dignified and religious woman, who turned a blind eye to her husband's constant infidelity and coped with pregnancy after pregnancy, miscarriages and still births. She was a traditional Queen who accepted her "lot in life" and her role as Queen of England. She knew that a king was expected to have mistresses and she also knew that her job was to ignore it and to carry on trying to provide the longed for male heir. How heartbroken she must have been when it became obvious that this was not going to happen, but how this heartbreak must have been magnified when she realised that her own lady-in-waiting, Anne Boleyn, was more than a mistress to the King! Catherine could never have anticipated this turn of events.

So how did Catherine treat Anne Boleyn?

There is no definitive answer to this question. George Cavendish, in his biography of Wolsey, would have us believe that Catherine's behaviour towards Anne was impeccable and that she "shewed([neither] to Mistress Anne, ne to the king) any spark or kind of grudge or displeasure...dissembled the same, having Mistress Anne in more estimation for the king's sake".

Wow, a true saint, but perhaps she was convinced at this stage that Anne was just another in a long line of royal mistresses and that she was no threat to a Queen with real royal blood. Other mistresses had come and gone, even ones like Elizabeth Blount who had actually provided the king with a son, so why would Anne be any different?

According to George Wyatt, Catherine actually tried to help Anne to resist Henry's advances and Anne remained loyal to her queen. Wyatt also talks of card games that Catherine instigated with Anne, in an apparent attempt to make Anne show her deformed finger (if you believe she had one!), and Catherine's famous remark to Anne "My lady Anne, you have good hap to stop at a king, but you are not like others, you will have all or none".

It is said that when of her ladies started talking ill of Anne Boleyn, Catherine told her off saying "Pray for her because the time would come when you shall pity and lament her case."

It seems that Catherine only realised the true threat that Anne was to her when she was made aware of Henry's secret plans for an annulment. In a letter to her nephew, the Holy Roman Emperor Charles, she begs Charles to plead her case to Pope Clement VII so that her marriage to Henry would be upheld and calls Anne Boleyn "the great scandal of Christendom". This is the first time we hear of Catherine saying a harsh word of Anne.

Catherine of Aragon was obviously distressed by the turn of events and showed dignity and strength of character in the way that she handled things. She was adamant that she was Henry's true wife and that her marriage to Henry's brother, Prince Arthur, had never been consummated and that Leviticus 20 verse 21 therefore did not apply. She fought tooth and nail for her marriage and the legitimacy of her daughter, seemingly without ever slandering Henry's new love.

Catherine and the Legatine Court

In May 1529, a legatine court was convened at Blackfriars in London to determine whether or not Henry VIII's marriage to Catherine of Aragon was lawful. This was Catherine's finest hour, in my opinion. On the 18th June, Catherine was called and instead of answering she dramatically approached the King, falling on her knees before him and making the following impassioned speech (according to George Cavendish, Wolsey's biographer):

"Sir, I beseech you, for all the loves that hath been between us, and for the love of God, let me have justice and right, take of me some pity and compassion, for I am a poor woman and stranger born out of your dominion, I have here no assured friend, and much less indifferent counsel; I flee to you as the head of justice within this realm.

Alas! Sir, wherein have I offended you, or what occasion have you of displeasure? Have I designed against your will and pleasure; intending (as I perceive) to put me from you? I take God and all the world to witness that I have been to you a true, humble and obedient wife, ever conformable to your will and pleasure, that never said or did any thing to the contrary thereof. This twenty years I have been your true wife or more. I have been your true wife, and by me ye have had divers children, although it hath pleased God to call them out of this world, which hath been no default in me. And when ye had me at the first, I take God to be my judge, I was a true maid.

If there be any just cause by the law that ye can allege against me, I am well content to depart, to my great shame; and if there be none, then here I must lowly beseech you, let me remain in my former estate.

The King your father was of such estimation throughout the world for his excellent wisdom, that he was called of all men the second Solomon; and my father Ferdinand, King of Spain, who was esteemed to be one of the wittiest princes that reigned in Spain, were both wise and excellent kings in wisdom and princely behaviour. They elected and gathered wise counsellors about them, who thought then the marriage between you and me good and lawful.

Therefore it is a wonder to hear what new inventions are invented against me. And cause me to stand to the order and judgment of this new court, wherein ye may do me much wrong, if ye intend any cruelty ; for ye may condemn me for lack of sufficient answer, having no indifferent counsel, but such as be assigned me with whose wisdom and learning I am not acquainted. Ye must consider that they cannot be indifferent counsellors for my part which be your subjects, and dare not, for your displeasure, disobey your will and intent. Therefore I most humbly require you, in the way of charity, and for the love of God, to spare me the extremity of this new court, until I may be advertised what way my friends in Spain will advise me to take. And if ye will not extend to me so much indifferent favour, your lo pleasure then be fulfilled, and to God I commit my cause!"

And with that, Catherine got up, made a curtsey to the King and left the hall.

I know I for one would have used this opportunity to lash out at the King, to publicise his adultery and his intentions to marry Anne Boleyn. Instead, Catherine showed her dignity and good breeding and acted the true Queen and wife. Catherine only spoke out against what Henry was basing the annulment on: the invalidity of the marriage (in his eyes). Not once did she mention Anne and the betrayal she must have felt from both her husband and her lady-in-waiting.

A Marriage Over

Even after the marriage was annulled and Henry eventually married a pregnant Anne in 1533, we have no record of Catherine speaking ill of Anne. We can only imagine how Catherine must have felt when she was stripped of the title "Queen" and given the title "Princess Dowager of Wales", expelled from court and commanded never to see her beloved daughter.

How awful her last three years of life must have been living a lonely life far from court, with a diminishing number of servants and in a state of poverty, compared to her previous life. Catherine became increasingly more pious, spending ever increasing time in prayer and she died just three years after Henry's marriage to Anne Boleyn. Some still believe that she died of a broken heart, although the official cause of death is thought to have been cancer. It is evident from Catherine's final letter to the King, allegedly written just before her death, that she never stopped loving him and that she still considered herself as his wife:-

"My most dear lord, king and husband,

The hour of my death now drawing on, the tender love I owe you forceth me, my case being such, to commend myself to you, and to put you in remembrance with a few words of the health and safeguard of your soul which you ought to prefer before all worldly matters, and before the care and pampering of your body, for the which you have cast me into many calamities and yourself into many troubles. For my part, I pardon you everything, and I wish to devoutly pray God that He will pardon you also. For the rest, I commend unto you our daughter Mary, beseeching you to be a good father unto her, as I have heretofore desired. I entreat you also, on behalf of my maids, to give them marriage portions, which is not much, they being but three. For all my other servants I solicit the wages due them, and a year more, lest they be unprovided for. Lastly, I make this vow, that mine eyes desire you above all things.

Katharine the Quene."

Anne is not mentioned but Catherine obviously feels that the King has sinned against God and is worried about his soul.

Anne Boleyn and
Catherine of Aragon – Part 2

Whatever our opinion on the matter, we cannot deny that Catherine of Aragon was treated despicably. She was a royal princess and Queen of England who deserved to be treated as such. All Catherine did was stick to her guns, insist that she was Henry's true wife (which she was) and refuse to be bullied by a King who wanted his own way. Catherine kept her dignity and acted in a Queenly manner and yet she was treated with cruelty.

The Treatment of Catherine of Aragon

Due to the fact that Catherine refused to accept that she was no longer queen, and refused to accept the validity of Henry VIII's marriage to Anne and the legitimacy of Princess Elizabeth, she was banished to Kimbolton Castle, a cold and remote property. Her maids were reduced to just three and her living allowance was cut drastically.

Sources suggest that she lived in just a small part of the castle, possibly just one room, and that she spent her last days wearing a hair shirt, praying for hours each day and only leaving her room to attend mass. She was forbidden from seeing, and even contacting, her daughter Mary and the last year of her life must have been one filled with heartbreak. It is no wonder that her health deteriorated rapidly and that she died on 7th January 1536 after weeks of illness.

Who's to Blame?

Who is to blame for this cruel treatment though?

Anne?

Henry?

Surely a man could not treat his wife of over 20 years in this way? Henry VIII had loved Catherine enough to rescue her from a precarious situation when her husband, Prince Arthur, had died, and their first few years of marriage seemed happy. Henry had trusted and respected Catherine enough to leave her in charge of England, fighting off the Scots while he dealt with France, and they had shared the joy of having a daughter and the heartbreak of losing child after child. Surely Henry could not be to blame!

See, it's easy for people to blame the wicked harlot, the "concubine", the "goggle eyed whore", or the other woman, for Catherine's suffering and her ultimate demise. No wonder Anne Boleyn is often portrayed as a cunning and spiteful woman who felt threatened by Catherine of Aragon and her daughter Mary and so wanted them out of the way. It was even suggested, by the Seymour alliance when Anne fell from favour, that Anne had planned to poison Catherine of Aragon, the Lady Mary and the Duke of Richmond (Henry Fitzroy)! Chapuys, the Imperial Ambassador, who loved to think ill of Anne, wrote of Catherine's death:-

"The Queen's illness began about five weeks ago, as I then wrote to your Majesty, and the attack was renewed on the morrow of Christmas day. It was a pain in the stomach, so violent that she could retain no food. I asked her physician several times if there was any suspicion of poison. He said he was afraid it was so, for after she had drunk some Welsh beer she had been worse, and that it must have been a slow and subtle poison for he could not discover evidences of simple and pure poison; but on opening her, indications will be seen. London, 9 Jan. 1536" LP x. 59

Chapuys was obviously implicating Anne in this, seeing as he had previously written of how he felt the lives of both Mary and Catherine were in danger from Anne and her followers.

The fact that Catherine's heart was black, when she was cut open for embalming, also fuelled the conspiracy theories as this was taken as a sign of poisoning. We now know that it was more likely that Catherine died of cancer, although her death could well have been hastened by a "broken heart". She was not poisoned and Anne Boleyn cannot be blamed for her death or labelled a murderess. But was Anne to blame for Catherine's treatment? Just how much influence did Anne have over Henry and how did she feel about Catherine?

Anne's Feelings

To be honest, I think Anne would have to be a saint not to harbour some resentment towards Catherine and Mary. We all know how it feels to go into a relationship where the ex is still lurking in the background. We would not be human if we did not want them to just disappear! Who can blame Anne for wanting Catherine and Mary to disappear into the background and pretend that they just didn't exist?!

There is actually not much evidence to testify to how Anne felt about Catherine. In "The Tudors", we see Anne having a fit about Catherine still making Henry's shirts (something she is said to have carried on doing) and Eric Ives makes the point that Chapuys often reports Anne complaining about Mary and making threats. But this was probably no more than Anne ranting, after all Anne was known for her quick temper. Here was Anne trying to be recognised as Queen and trying to get her daughter recognised as heir to the throne, can we blame her for her frustration and resentment of Catherine and Mary, and of the threat to her daughter's future throne?

Anne had famously said of Mary:

"She is my death and I am hers; so I will take care that she shall not laugh at me after my death" LP ix.873

So she obviously saw Mary as a very real threat.

Alison Weir points out how ironic it is that Anne thought that things would be better when Catherine died, yet Catherine's death actually brought about Anne's fall. With Catherine's death, Henry VIII was free to get rid of Anne and move on to another woman (Jane Seymour) without being forced to return to his "real" wife, Catherine. Henry could not have set Anne aside while Catherine lived.

It is obvious that Anne felt great relief on hearing the news of the death of Catherine of Aragon – her rival was gone, hurrah! Her relief and happiness are shown by the fact that she rewarded the messenger with a gift and that she and Henry celebrated, BUT who wore yellow and what did this mean?

There are different accounts of Henry and Anne's celebration of Catherine's death. One account has Henry crying out:

"God be praised that we are free from all suspicion of war!"

The next day, both Anne Boleyn and Henry VIII appeared at court dressed "from top to toe" in "joyful yellow" and "triumphantly paraded" their daughter Elizabeth to church. However, it is not really clear who was dressed in yellow that day.

Eustace Chapuys, the Imperial Ambassador, reported to his master, Charles V that "On the following day, Sunday, the King was clad all over in yellow, from top to toe, except the white feather he had in his bonnet, and the Little Bastard was conducted to mass with trumpets and other great triumphs", making no mention of Anne. The chronicler Edward Hall, however, puts Anne in yellow, writing that "Quene Anne ware yelowe for the mournyng."

The Catholic recusant Nicholas Sander, writing in Elizabeth I's reign, reported that "The king could not refrain from tears when he read the letter [Catherine's last letter to him], but Anne Boleyn, instead of putting on mourning on the day of Catherine's funeral, put on a yellow dress."

But then Sander quotes Hall as his source, so he is certainly not a new source for this information.

There is much controversy about Henry and/or Anne wearing the colour yellow because in England yellow is generally linked with happiness, not mourning. Some suggest that yellow was a mourning colour in Spain at this time, although I have been unable to find evidence of this, so it is difficult to figure out the motivation behind wearing this colour. Perhaps Henry VIII knew that he would be seen as a hypocrite for wearing black when he had treated Catherine so abominably and perhaps this wearing of yellow was out of respect for her. There are reports that both Henry and Anne wept in private over Catherine's death, but I have been unable to find solid evidence of this.

So, we have no real evidence of how Anne felt about Catherine and Catherine's death, but we can see, with hindsight, that it was the beginning of the end for Anne.

Conclusion

I apologise for my ramblings but I will conclude with saying that I think that the only person responsible for Catherine's suffering and ill-treatment was King Henry VIII.

Whether or not you believe that Anne had some magical hold or influence over him, Henry was big and bad enough to make his own decisions. He ordered Catherine to be banished from Court, he sent her away to Kimbolton and gave her rooms to Anne, and he forbade her to see or contact Mary. Henry was ultimately responsible and he punished Catherine for defying him. Catherine of Aragon had the nerve (how Henry saw it) to refuse to go quietly. She had humiliated the King at the Legatine Court with her passionate speech, she refused to accept the annulment, she carried on referring to herself as Queen and seeking advice from the Pope and Holy Roman Emperor, she had the tenacity to refuse to go to a convent and she was stirring up trouble for Henry and his new wife. Catherine had to be brought down a peg or two and shown who was boss – he, Henry, would show her!

I truly believe, whatever "The Tudors" or historical fiction would have us believe, that Henry was in ultimate control and that he is the only one to blame for Catherine's poor treatment and death. Anne was the excuse, not the cause.

Notes and Sources

- The Life and Death of Anne Boleyn, Eric Ives
- Letters and Papers, Foreign and Domestic, Henry VIII
- The Six Wives of Henry VIII, Alison Weir
- Hall's Chronicle, Edward Hall
- Rise and Growth of the Anglican Schism, Nicholas Sander

Did Anne Boleyn Commit Incest with Her Brother?

This article was inspired by the controversy over the publication of G W Bernard's book "Anne Boleyn: Fatal Attractions", and his idea that Anne Boleyn may have been partially guilty of the charges against her, and also the continuing popularity of "The Other Boleyn Girl" in which Anne and George commit incest.

Most historians these days are sympathetic to Anne's cause and believe that Anne Boleyn, Mark Smeaton, Sir Henry Norris, Sir William Brereton, Sir Francis Weston and Anne's brother George Boleyn, Lord Rochford, were framed in a successful attempt to get rid of Anne and bring down the whole Boleyn faction. However, there are those who think there is truth in the charges against Anne, that there's no smoke without a fire and that she was partially guilty.

In his article, "The Fall of Anne Boleyn", which was published in 1991, G W Bernard writes of how Anne Boleyn's fall was not the result of a selfish king wanting to get rid of his unwanted wife, or a faction battle or even Cromwell plotting against her. Instead, he believes that it was caused by an argument between one of Anne's ladies and her brother. He concludes that it is likely that Anne and at least some of those accused with her were guilty of the charges against them. He gives various possible explanations:-

- Henry's on-off impotence - This may have caused a desperate Anne to look to other men to father an heir to the throne.

- Anne's sexual appetite

- Her jealousy of the King's affairs

Bernard writes of how it is an analysis of the historical evidence, not prejudice against Anne, that has led to him believing that Anne may have been unfaithful and that her behaviour was discovered when one of her ladies had a quarrel with her brother. When her infidelity came to light then her fall was surely inevitable.

Bernard goes on to say that we may judge Henry's treatment of Anne as harsh but that it was understandable. He sees Henry as being in complete control of the situation and not the victim of any type of manipulation. Anne fell because she was unfaithful.

An article in the 23rd February 2010 Daily Mail discussed how G W Bernard believes that a French poem written just a few days after Anne Boleyn's execution in May 1536 reveals the truth about the Queen's infidelities. According to Bernard, the 1,000 line poem written by Lancelot de Carles, secretary to the French ambassador, calls Anne a "common whore" and names Mark Smeaton, Henry Norris and Anne's brother George as her lovers. Here is an extract from an English translation:-

> "She never stops her daily round
> Lubricious fun with one by one
> Just like a common whore
> When one is over for the day
> Another comes along on time
> And then another...
> Norris and Mark could not deny
> That they have often passed with her
> Many a night"

Professor Bernard believes that this poem can be backed up with evidence and should not be discounted as just a salacious literary work. In the poem, de Carles writes of how the accusations of infidelity against Anne first came to light in a quarrel between a pregnant lady of the Queen's privy chamber and her brother, who was a privy councillor. In this argument, the brother accuses his sister of being promiscuous and she replies that her behaviour is nothing compared to her mistress the Queen who is committing adultery with her own brother. The sister then goes on to say that Smeaton and Norris have been seduced by Anne's "caresses".

Bernard identifies the pregnant lady-in-waiting as the Countess of Worcester, a woman who has often been talked of as providing evidence against Anne Boleyn and who is identified in a 16th century letter as Anne's main accuser. Eric Ives, in "The Life and Death of Anne Boleyn", writes of how John Hussee wrote to Lord Lisle and listed Anne Cobham, "my Lady Worcester" and "one maid more" as sources of information against Anne. Ives then goes on to explain that Elizabeth Browne, Countess of Worcester, was the sister of Sir Anthony Browne of the privy chamber and that Thomas Cromwell presented Lady Worcester's evidence as the first evidence of Anne's guilt.

Bernard concludes that the fact that Anne Boleyn's ladies-in-waiting knew of and spoke of their mistress's affairs make her infidelities more believable. Although other historians have discounted the idea that a queen could have committed adultery, he argues that it could have happened if her ladies were involved and "complicit", just like in the case of Catherine Howard. Historians do not question Catherine's guilt so why, asks Bernard, should the charges against Anne be dismissed so easily?

But why would Anne risk everything for these affairs?

Professor Bernard believes that she took lovers because of Henry VIII's on-off problems with impotence and that the affairs were her way of getting pregnant and providing the King with an heir.

In his report of 1991, Bernard cites the French poem as evidence against Anne, along with Mark Smeaton's confession, Anne's flirtatious behaviour with Norris and Weston, and the talk of Norris being Elizabeth's father. Bernard believes that Anne committed adultery with Norris and Smeaton, and could also have been involved with the others. He points out that other men, like Wyatt, and Page, were questioned and imprisoned, but not tried and executed. He believes that this reinforces the idea that the accusations against Anne and the men were not "indiscriminate" and that Henry VIII and his ministers did weigh up the evidence carefully.

The Case for the Defence

If I say "tommyrot" and "poppycock", people won't take me very seriously will they? But that's how I feel!

There is nothing new in Bernard producing the poetry of Lancelot de Carles as evidence against Anne Boleyn in his new book, particularly as it is mentioned in his report of 1991. Eric Ives also quotes de Carles as saying that Anne would line up her men, her "mignons" at night and that these men included Norris, Smeaton and her brother, but he dismisses it as "moonshine", as rubbish, just like the evidence in the indictments. He also discounts the argument between Lady Worcester and her brother as evidence, believing it to be an exaggeration of an argument where Browne was criticising his sister's behaviour and she was simply lashing out saying that she was no more flirtatious than her mistress, the Queen.

Ives also notes that Justice Spelman, a man who heard all of the evidence against Anne, made no mention of Lady Worcester and that said that "all of the evidence was of bawdry and lechery". If Lady Worcester's evidence was so damning then why was she not mentioned?

Alison Weir, in "The Lady in the Tower", also mentions de Carles and the Countess of Worcester story and in her notes on Chapter 4 Weir mentions that the Countess may well have been persuaded by relatives to betray the Queen and that she was worried about the money she had secretly borrowed from Anne. Weir also wonders if de Carles got his facts mixed up in naming Lady Worcester as the source of the incest story when most sources agree that this story came only from Jane Parker, Lady Rochford, the wife of George Boleyn.

One interesting theory in Bernard's report "The Fall of Anne Boleyn", is the suggestion that the Countess of Worcester was Thomas Cromwell's mistress!

To use a "gossipy" poem, written by a man who surely would have been fed propaganda by Thomas Cromwell, as evidence strong enough to convict and execute a person just does not make sense to me. If this poem was based on fact, if Lady Worcester really gave the crown concrete evidence, then I need answers to the following questions:-

- Why were no ladies-in-waiting convicted alongside Anne Boleyn? – In the case of Catherine Howard, Lady Rochford was convicted and executed for being an accomplice, a go-between and helping Catherine meet Culpeper, so why weren't Anne's ladies charged as accomplices? They would have been helping the Queen to commit treason and so would have been traitors too.

- Why don't the dates in the indictments make sense? – If there was evidence of Anne's infidelity then the dates cited should have surely made sense. Instead, as Eric Ives points out, the majority of the charges can be disproved because there is proof that Anne and/or the men weren't even at the place mentioned.

- Why wasn't Henry VIII completely distraught like he was when he heard of Catherine Howard's infidelities? – He wept in front of his council when he was given evidence against Catherine, yet he had pursued Anne for seven years, broke with Rome to marry her, been excommunicated by the Pope, been married to her for three years and yet he seemed indifferent to the allegations against his wife.

When talking of G W Bernard's past opinion that Anne and at least some of the men were guilty, Ives writes that there is no evidence to back up that theory. He points out that the Crown began breaking up her household two days before her trial and that Chapuys records that Henry told Jane, on the morning of his wife's trial that Anne would be found guilty. It was a set-up, Anne had no chance.

Conclusion

Gossip, slander and propaganda, that's all it seems to me. I don't put Anne Boleyn up on a pedestal, I don't believe that she was a martyr or saint, but I do believe that she was innocent of all of the charges against her, that she was a victim of a political struggle and that her death was a tragic example of injustice and should be classed as murder, along with the deaths of George Boleyn, Mark Smeaton, Sir Henry Norris, Sir William Brereton and Sir Francis Weston.

There is no way that this intelligent woman, who had waited so long to be Queen, would risk everything, her crown and her life, for some fun on the side. Even if she was desperate for a child, she knew that the child needed to be Henry's, and that she couldn't risk the child being a spitting image of Henry Norris, the King's best friend! And to accuse her of incest is to deny the strong faith that both Anne and George had. Incest was an abomination, an offence against God, and both Anne and George were highly religious. They were reformers who risked their lives by owning reformist texts and tracts at times when people were being killed as heretics for owning such things, they would not have risked their souls in such a way.

OK, I'll get off my soapbox now!!

Notes and Sources

- "Anne Boleyn DID have an affair with her brother: The poem that 'proves' the adultery of Henry VIII's queen" – An article from "The Daily Mail", 23rd February 2011
- "The Fall of Anne Boleyn" – A report by G W Bernard, published in 1991 in "The English Historical Review".
- "Anne Boleyn: Fatal Attractions", G W Bernard
- "The Life and Death of Anne Boleyn", Eric Ives
- "The Lady in the Tower", Alison Weir

Did Anne Boleyn Dig Her Own Grave?

I apologise for the "inflammatory" title but blame David Starkey as it was he who got me wondering!

When I watched Starkey's "Henry VIII: Mind of a Tyrant", the episode on Anne Boleyn really got me thinking if Anne Boleyn has to take some responsibility for her downfall and execution. In it, Starkey talked about how Anne's forthright character and ability to say "no" to Henry, which had been so attractive in a mistress, was not what Henry wanted in a wife. Starkey talked of how Henry could no longer tolerate Anne's nagging and jealousy, and this must have affected his feelings towards her.

In her book "The Other Tudors: Henry VIII's Mistresses and Bastards", Philippa Jones talks about how Henry VIII had unrealistic expectations of women. He wanted a perfect love and a perfect woman, a woman like his mother, but no woman could possibly measure up to his ideal.

He was attracted to Anne because she was so different to the usual English Rose. She was dark haired and dark eyed, she exuded sex appeal, she was intelligent and could debate subjects like theology with Henry. She was feisty and would stand up to him. The couple were known for their passionate arguments, and their passionate "reunions", but it seems that Henry expected Anne to change once she was Queen. It appears that Henry wanted to "have his cake and eat it" – own a passionate woman but also a woman who was like his mother, or former wife, a woman he could control and master. Anne was not this sort of woman.

We know, from Eustace Chapuys the Imperial ambassador, that Anne Boleyn was jealous of Henry VIII showing attention to other women. Who can blame her when her position relied on keeping Henry's interest and love? Chapuys writes of how Anne showed jealousy and had words with the King and that he replied that she should "shut her eyes and endure" and that he could lower her as quickly as he had made her rise. What a threat but, if you look at it through Henry's eyes, a king was expected to have mistresses and dalliances, and a queen was supposed to turn a blind eye, just as Catherine of Aragon had done.

So, what mistakes did Anne make that could be responsible for her downfall and tragic end?

- She nagged Henry – Henry wanted to be in control and live his own life, he certainly did not want a wife who nagged him! A documentary entitled "Days that Shook the World: The Execution of Anne Boleyn" states that there were two reasons for Anne Boleyn's fall: her "refusal to curb the bold manners he once found so attractive" and her failure to provide a son.

- She showed her jealousy and berated Henry for flirting with other women, like Jane Seymour – Chapuys describes Anne's "intense rage" over Henry's behaviour with Jane Seymour.

- Anne made an enemy of Thomas Cromwell - Overnight, Cromwell went from being Anne Boleyn's greatest ally to being her greatest enemy. If Anne had not argued with Cromwell over the dissolution of the monasteries and shown that she was pro-French and against an imperial alliance then Cromwell may well have stayed her supporter. We now know that Cromwell's plans for an imperial-English alliance, and his fear that Anne would lead to his downfall, led to him conspiring against Anne.

- Anne incriminated herself – Cromwell cooked up a plot that Simon Schama calls "pure devilry", a plan that took advantage of the King's paranoia, but, at first, he did not have any real and credible evidence to convict Anne. As well as a confession of adultery with the Queen from Mark Smeaton, which may have been gained through torture, Cromwell was fortunate enough to get evidence from the Queen herself. In her fright and confusion in the Tower, Anne rambled and talked about possible events that could have been misconstrued. She spoke of episodes of courtly love – of Francis Weston declaring his love for her, of reprimanding Smeaton who had made eyes and "love sighs" at her and of reprimanding Henry Norris for looking for "dead man's shoes" – but all these entirely innocent shows of courtly love that Anne spoke of were fed back to Cromwell by Lord Kingston and twisted into orgies and adultery.

- Anne did not provide a male heir – She promised Henry a male heir but did not deliver on her promise.

- She openly supported the "New Religion" – Anne had an English Bible that she encouraged her ladies to read and shared heretical books with the King. She made many enemies because of this.

- Anne made an enemy of Mary – Her fear and jealousy of Catherine of Aragon and Princess/Lady Mary led to her alienating Mary and making an enemy of her.

- Anne believed in Henry's love for her – Anne was naive enough to believe that Henry's love and passion for her could last for ever. Who can blame her? Henry moved Heaven and Earth to get Anne!

- Anne set a dangerous precedent – Anne had shown ladies at court what could be achieved. She, herself, had risen from a lady-in-waiting to usurp the Queen's place and now somebody could do that to her. No longer did ladies just have to pin their hopes on being a mistress, they could be queen!

- Anne was reckless – David Starkey talks of Anne's ambition and recklessness. Was she over ambitious and too reckless?

However long I consider these mistakes that Anne is said to have been made, I can never convince myself that Anne Boleyn was responsible for her fall and execution. Simon Schama believes Cromwell to be "the author" of Anne's fall and he only acted because he feared for his life and knew that the King had fallen in love with Jane.

In my opinion, Henry VIII has to take responsibility for

Anne's cruel and tragic end. He had warned her that he could drag her down as quickly as he had raised her, and he was true to this promise. Henry VIII had tired of Anne, felt betrayed by her (because she had broken her promise to give him a son) and now wanted to move on to another woman. Henry's priority was the succession. Unfortunately for Anne, divorce was out of the question and another ending was required – death.

We now know, from historical evidence and research, that Anne Boleyn was innocent of all charges and was executed an innocent woman. She had her faults, like any of us, but she did not deserve to die a traitor to the crown and did not deserve Henry's hatred or worse, indifference.

Did Henry VIII Commit Bigamy
When He Married Anne Boleyn?

This post is inspired by two long and heated, debates on The Anne Boleyn Files forum regarding Henry VIII being a bigamist and also Anne Boleyn being a home-wrecker.

Nikki from Texas got the ball rolling on the bigamy topic by pointing out that Henry VIII married a pregnant Anne Boleyn and THEN, a few months later, his marriage to Catherine of Aragon was annulled. Very true, let's look at the facts:-

- 11th June 1509 – Henry VIII marries Catherine of Aragon.
- 14th November 1532 (St Erkenwald's Day) or the 25th January 1533 (or both!) – Henry VIII marries Anne Boleyn.
- November 1532 – Henry VIII and Anne Boleyn consummate their relationship, either while still in France or on their return home from seeking Francis I's blessing.
- February 1533 – Anne Boleyn speaks of craving apples, she is pregnant.
- March 1533 – Henry VIII's court preachers proclaim the "virtues and secret merits" of Anne Boleyn while proclaiming that his marriage to Catherine is invalid.
- 26th March 1533 – Convocation is asked to pronounce on the validity of a papal dispensation allowing a man to marry his brother's widow.
- 30th March 1533 – Thomas Cranmer is consecrated as Archbishop of Canterbury.
- End of March 1533 – Anne Boleyn's royal household is formed.
- 1st April 1533 – Cranmer takes the chair in the upper house of Convocation and within a few days "large majorities" are

in favour of two propositions: 1) That Prince Arthur had "carnally known" Catherine of Aragon and 2) That the Pope had no power to issue a dispensation allowing Catherine to marry Henry VIII and rule in Henry VIII's favour.

- Wednesday 9th April 1533, Holy Week – Catherine is told of her new title, Dowager Princess of Wales, and informed that Henry VIII is married to Anne Boleyn.

- Good Friday, 11th April 1533 – Henry VIII informs the court that Anne Boleyn is now Queen.

- Easter Saturday, 12th April 1533 – Anne attends Mass as Queen.

- 10th May 1533 – Archbishop Cranmer opens a special court at Dunstable for the annulment proceedings.

- 23rd May 1533 – Cranmer's court rules that the marriage between Henry VIII and Catherine of Aragon was against the will of God and declares the marriage null and void.

- 28th May 1533 – Cranmer declares the marriage between Henry VIII and Anne Boleyn valid.

- 29th May 1533 – The coronation pageantry begins.

- 1st June 1533 – Anne Boleyn is crowned Queen at Westminster Abbey.

Definition of Bigamy

bigamy - big·a·my/bigəmē/
Noun: The act of marrying while already married to another person.

Did Henry VIII Commit Bigamy? - Yes

If we just look at the facts above with our 21st century eyes and ideals then it is easy for us to declare Henry VIII a bigamist. After all, he married his second wife, Anne Boleyn, a few months before his first marriage to Catherine of Aragon was annulled. It is clear that he went through with the act of marrying Anne Boleyn when he was already married to Catherine. He was a bigamist.

Did Henry VIII Commit Bigamy? - No

We now have to look at the situation through Henry VIII's eyes. Here was a man who had been troubled for a few years about the fact that his marriage to Catherine of Aragon was contrary to Biblical Law, in that it contravened Biblical Law:-

"And if a man shall take his brother's wife, it [is] an unclean thing: he hath uncovered his brother's nakedness; they shall be childless." Leviticus 20:21

While Henry and Catherine had not been childless, they had not been blessed with a living son and heir, so Henry truly believed that there was something about the marriage that God was not happy with. He got it in his head that the miscarriages/stillbirths were due to sin, due to the fact that Catherine had married him after already having been married to his brother. As for the papal dispensation, well, Henry believed that Pope Julius II had made a grave error trying to dispense a law of this nature and that Pope Clement VII must set it right.

While it is easy for us to look at Henry's justification for the annulment of his first marriage as a great excuse to get out of it and move on, it is clear that he was actually troubled by this. He came to believe that the marriage was wrong in God's eyes and should never have taken place. David Starkey writes of how, during the 7 years of Henry's quest for an annulment, the basic premise of Henry's case did not change and he stuck to his argument, he was convinced.

In Henry VIII's eyes, his marriage to Catherine was invalid, so he was not married. Although it was important for him to get the marriage officially annulled, so that any offspring would be legitimate in everyone's eyes, he had no qualms about marrying Anne Boleyn before the official annulment. To him, it was valid whenever it took place. The fact that Anne became pregnant so quickly made him sure that God was blessing their union.

Conclusion

Phew! What a minefield!

It is easy to be black and white about things like this but, at the end of the day, we have to see things through the eyes of those concerned. Obviously, Catherine always believed that she was Henry's true wife and never accepted the annulment, but Henry VIII felt that he was God's appointed sovereign and therefore what he said went. He believed his first marriage was invalid, he believed that God did not recognise it as a true marriage and he felt vindicated by the rulings of Convocation and Cranmer's court. Of course, he then goes on to annul his marriage to Anne Boleyn in 1536, but that's another story...

Notes and Sources

- Six Wives: The Queens of Henry VIII, David Starkey
- The Life and Death of Anne Boleyn, Eric Ives, p164
- A Timeline of Anne Boleyn's Relationship with Henry VIII 1528-1533, Claire Ridgway on The Anne Boleyn Files website
- Merriam-Webster Online Dictionary

Anne Boleyn and Henry VIII's Marriage: Doomed from the Start?

Anne Boleyn and Henry VIII got married in a secret ceremony on the 25th January 1533, nearly 7 years after Henry declared his love for Anne at the 1526 Shrovetide joust. But what happened after they married?

We know that the marriage ended tragically, just over three years later, but was it always doomed? Were Anne and Henry unhappy from the moment they tied the knot?

Yes, it was doomed

- Henry's passion quickly abated – Alison Weir believes that the marriage was not a blissful one and that Henry had not been all that kind to Anne.[1] She continues by saying that Henry's passion for Anne quickly abated and that he started being unfaithful to her during her first pregnancy, warning her that she had to "shut her eyes" and put up with it as Catherine had. He warned Anne that he could bring her down as quickly as he had raised her.[2] He turned from the earnest, desperate lover to an unkind and fickle husband.

- The thrill of the chase was gone – The King had waited for seven years to make Anne his wife and these years of waiting may well have taken their toll on Anne and Henry. They had both fought so hard for the marriage so was it a bit of an anti-climax when it finally happened? Eustace Chapuys reported in August 1533[3] that the relationship had cooled and that Henry's flirtations and Anne's jealousy were causing problems.

- Anne's "shrewish" nature – Alison Weir writes of how Anne had become shrewish, haughty, proud and moody.[4] David Starkey in his TV series "The Six Wives of Henry VIII", talks of tensions in the marriage caused by Anne not being able to make the transition from mistress to wife and queen. Her personality, which had been exciting and acceptable before their marriage, was not what Henry wanted in his Queen and he made that clear.[5]

- Henry "was no good in bed"[6] – David Starkey says that Anne had her complaints about Henry too and apparently told a lady of her bedchamber that her husband was no good in bed.

- Anne was in an impossible situation from the very start – She had attracted the King with her personality, her wit and her "sexual panache"[7], but it was this same personality that was now putting her in danger of losing him. She was also jealous of his dalliances with other women and could not help but react angrily. The relationship became more and more volatile as Anne felt more and more threatened and Henry tired of Anne's moods and what he saw as irrational behaviour.

- Evidence of Eustace Chapuys, the Imperial Ambassador - As early as August and September 1533, he reported "with the long time the King has been away from the Lady, that he has begun to repent." In 1534, Chapuys wrote of how Anne wanted to send a beautiful woman away from court because Henry was paying her attention[8].

- Henry's infidelity – Charles V wrote in August 1533: "It is said that the English nobles are ill-disposed towards Anne on account of her pride and the insolence and bad conduct of her brothers and relations. For the same reason the King's affection for her is less than it was. He now shows himself in love with another lady, and many nobles are assisting him in the affair."[9] BUT Ives notes that this letter is actually dated wrong and is from autumn 1534, so not a few months after the marriage.

No, it wasn't

- George Wyatt's evidence – George Wyatt, grandson of the poet Thomas Wyatt, wrote "And thus we see they lived and loved, tokens of increasing love perpetually increasing between them. Her mind brought him forth the rich treasures of love of piety, love of truth, love of learning. Her body yielded him the fruits of marriage, inestimable pledges of her faith and loyal love."[10]

- Just lovers' quarrels – Although Chapuys reported in September 1533 that Anne was "full of jealousy, and not without cause" and that a heated argument had led to Henry not speaking to Anne for two or three days, Chapuys was quick to say that "no doubt these things are lovers' quarrels, to which we must not attach too great importance". G W Bernard points out that reports of quarrels are simply evidence of a "sunshine and storms" relationship, rather than as signs of the end Even Chapuys tempered his accounts of arguments caused by Anne's jealous by explaining that they were just lovers' quarrels and so should not be taken seriously. Also, there is far more evidence of the couple being happy, than of them arguing.[11]

- The many reports of Anne and Henry's happiness – G W Bernard writes that they were often reported as being "merry" and that these types of reports carried on as late as autumn 1535.[12] Sir William Kingston commented in a letter to Lord Lisle on the 20th July 1533 that "The King and Queen are well and merry"[13], Sir Anthony Browne wrote to Cromwell on the 24th July 1533 "Today I received your letter dated London, 17 July, with news of the good health of the King and Queen and my other friends",[14] "I never saw the King merrier than he is now" was what Sir John Russell wrote to Lord Lisle on the 6th Aug 1533[15] and George Tayllour wrote to Lady Lisle on the 19th August 1533, saying "The King and Queen are in good health and merry."[16]

- Reports of the King being besotted with Anne – "They say in Flanders "that the King is abused by the new Queen, and that his gentlemen goeth daily a playing where they woll, and his Grace abides by her all the day long, and dare not go out for the rumor of the people."[17] Eric Ives writes of how in autumn 1533, Anne's ladies were saying that Henry had claimed that he would prefer to go door-to-door begging alms than to give up his wife.[18]

- Reports of happiness as late as January 1536 – Although Chapuys reports that Henry had not been speaking much to Anne before her miscarriage in January 1536, G W Bernard states that we have reports of the couple rejoicing over Catherine's death, Henry parading Elizabeth around happily and jousting. When Anne did miscarry a son, Bernard points out Chapuys' report that Anne "attributed the misfortune to two causes: first, the King's fall; and, secondly, that the love she bore him was far greater than that of the late Queen, so that her heart broke when she saw that he loved others." According to Chapuys "the King was much grieved" and stayed with Anne.[19] Anne was also quick to reassure her ladies by saying that she would soon be pregnant again. Bernard concludes that the evidence suggests that the relationship was volatile and may have "cooled" in spring 1536, but that this is not evidence of the King giving up on Anne or the miscarriage being the end.[20]

- The King's infidelity does not mean that he was falling out of love with Anne – Although we have reports of Henry having flirtations and Anne plotting with Lady Rochford to remove one damsel from court, because she had caught Henry's eye, we have to remember that it was a King's prerogative to take mistresses. This was common when the queen was pregnant. Even Jane Seymour may have been a passing flirtation if events had not conspired to bring Anne down.

- Henry was committed to Anne – G W Bernard comments

that even in early 1536, Henry was committed to Anne and to having her recognised as his Queen. He did not discard her after Catherine of Aragon's death, safe in the knowledge that he would not be forced back into his first marriage, instead he kept working to get his marriage accepted and Anne recognised as his true wife. For example, he summoned Chapuys, the imperial ambassador, to court in April 1536, just weeks before Anne's execution, and managed to get him to recognise Anne. Bernard concludes that this must mean that Henry had no intention of discarding Anne at this point and that this was reinforced by him dissolving the Reformation Parliament in April, suggesting that he did not expect it to have to deal with any business concerning his marriage or a potential annulment.[21]

- Chapuys was a gossip, read too much into situations and got things wrong – Eric Ives talks of how Chapuys' information was often tainted, in that it came from Anne's enemies, and that he did get things wrong. Also, when Chapuys wrote of the new lady being "the damsel whom the king has been accustomed to serve", Ives points out that the phrase "accustomed to serve" is the language of courtly love and chivalry, so is not describing a real, serious relationship. Ives concludes that Henry was simply using this damsel as a substitute for his wife while she recovered from her miscarriage.[22]

- A passionate and volatile relationship – The thing is that Anne and Henry were lovers, not just King and Queen. Their relationship had grown out of love, not out of diplomacy. They had lovers' quarrels and their relationship was stormy at times.

- The relationship suffered tension from external factors which worsened as time went on – It is no wonder that Anne and Henry argued when their relationship was put under so much pressure and stress. Eric Ives and David Starkey both talk of the tension caused by factors such as Mary refusing to recognise Anne and Anne being blamed for Mary's treatment, Anne's unpopularity and the hostility towards her, Anne being blamed for the religious and political changes which resulted in bloodshed, Anne's struggle to give Henry a son and Anne's French connections. David Loades writes that Anne was just like Cardinal Wolsey in that her position relied entirely upon the King's favour and that this favour was in jeopardy by the end of 1534[24] due to the constant tension caused by the behaviour of Mary and Anne's unpopularity.

My Own Thoughts

Having read through contemporary reports and the various arguments put forward by eminent historians, I have to agree with Eric Ives' view that Henry and Anne's relationship was one where "storm followed sunshine, sunshine followed storm". Both Anne and Henry were passionate people with hot tempers. They argued passionately and made up just as passionately. They might exchange cross words and sulk for a few days but it would all blow over and was quickly forgotten. Even Chapuys, a man who was always eager to report any breach in their relationship and any hope for a reconciliation between the King and Catherine, put their arguments down to "lovers' quarrels, to which we must not attach too great importance".

I do not believe that Anne Boleyn and Henry VIII's relationship was doomed from the start but I think that it finally failed for the following reasons:-

- Anne's jealousy, which was a result of her precarious position as Henry's lover, not just his queen

- Henry's belief that he was cursed – He began to wonder if his lack of a male heir was a sign that the marriage was cursed

- External factors which put pressure on Anne and Henry and which caused tension between them

- Anne's enemies 'drip-feeding' Henry and making him doubt Anne in May 1536 and causing him to move against her – They knew Henry's vulnerabilities and his paranoia
- Anne's inability to provide Henry with a son

Notes and Sources

1. The Lady in the Tower, Alison Weir, p10

2. LP vi.1069, quoted in Weir

3. LP vi.975

4. Weir, p11

5. The Six Wives of Henry VIII, David Starkey on Channel 4

6. Ibid.

7. The Six Wives of Henry VIII, David Loades, p68-69

8. LP vii.1193

9. LP vi.1054

10. The Life of Anne Boleigne, George Wyatt, in The Life of Cardinal Wolsey: Volume II, George Cavendish

11. The Fall of Anne Boleyn, article by G W Bernard in English Historical Review, 1991

12. Ibid

13. LP vi.879

14. LP vi.891

15. LP vi.948

16. LP vi.1004

17. LP vi. 1065

18. The Life and Death of Anne Boleyn, Eric Ives, p193

19. Bernard, LP x.351

20. Ibid.

21. Ibid.

22. Ives, p195

23. David Loades, p68-69

Anne Boleyn's Ladies-in-Waiting

I am often asked about Anne Boleyn's ladies-in-waiting, so I thought it would be good to write a post giving the low-down on some of her ladies. I apologise if I have missed any, but here is some information on the ladies mentioned in the primary sources as serving Anne Boleyn at one time or another.

Anne Gainsford, Lady Zouche

Anne Gainsford is thought to have joined Anne Boleyn's household before Anne married Henry, probably around 1528, and she became one of the Queen's ladies-in-waiting in 1533. She became Lady Zouche on her marriage to Sir George Zouche in 1533 and it is said that the couple had eight children.

It was Anne, or Nan as she was known, to whom Anne Boleyn lent her copy of Tyndale's "The Obedience of a Christian Men" and when her fiancé, George Zouche, stole it off her it fell into Wolsey's hands and was shown to the King. It was also Anne Zouche who told George Wyatt, Thomas Wyatt's grandson, about Thomas Wyatt stealing Anne's jewel from around her neck.[1] Anne Gainsford was also the lady to whom Anne Boleyn showed what Eric Ives[2] calls a "poison-pen drawing" and what Anne Boleyn referred to as "a book of prophecy". It had been left in Anne's apartments. The drawing depicted a male figure labelled with an "H" and two female figures labelled "K" and "A". The "A" figure was missing her head. When Anne Gainsford was shown the book, it is said that she commented "If I thought it true, though he were an emperor, I would not myself marry him". Her mistress, on the other hand, dismissed it, saying "I think the book a bauble, yet for the hope I have that the realm may be happy by my issue, I am resolved to have him whatsoever might become of me."[3]

Anne went on to serve Jane Seymour after the fall of Anne Boleyn.

Trivia: Bess of Hardwick lived for a time with Anne Gainsford, Lady Zouche.

Elizabeth (Bess) Holland

Elizabeth Holland was the daughter of the secretary of Thomas Howard, 3rd Duke of Norfolk, and she became the Duke's mistress in 1527 when she was working as a laundress to his wife, Elizabeth Howard. When Elizabeth Howard complained to her husband about Bess being his mistress, it is said that he beat his wife savagely. Bess was the Duke's mistress for around 8 years.

The Imperial Ambassador, Eustace Chapuys, mentions Bess as the Duke's mistress and as one of Anne Boleyn's ladies in a letter dated September 1533.[4]

Bess went on to serve Jane Seymour and was one of the ladies in Jane's funeral procession.

Trivia: Bess gave evidence against her former lover, the Duke of Norfolk, and his son, Henry Howard, Earl of Surrey, which led to Surrey being executed and Norfolk only escaping execution because the King died before his scheduled execution.

Margery Horsman

Margery Horsman served as lady-in-waiting to Catherine of Aragon, Anne Boleyn and Jane Seymour. Eric Ives[5] believes that the anonymous lady listed with Anne Cobham and Lady Worcester as being sources of information against Anne Boleyn in 1536 must have been Margery. After Anne's execution, Margery went on to serve Jane Seymour and in 1537 she married Sir Michael Lyster and became Keeper of the Queen's Jewels jointly with him.

Jane Parker
(also known as Jane Boleyn and Lady Rochford)

Jane was Anne Boleyn's sister-in-law, being married to Anne's brother, George Boleyn, Lord Rochford. Jane Parker was the daughter of Henry Parker, 8th Baron Morley and his wife Alice St

John. She married George Boleyn, Anne Boleyn's brother, in late 1524 or early 1525, and went on to become one of her sister-in-laws attendants.

Jane is often blamed for being a factor in the downfall of her husband and Anne Boleyn. It is said that she gave evidence against the siblings, causing them to be found guilty of incest. However, we do not know what Jane said when she was interrogated by Thomas Cromwell, apart from the fact that she spoke of Anne and George's indiscretion in discussing Henry VIII's sexual inadequacies.

Jane went on to serve three more of Henry VIII's wives: Jane Seymour, Anne of Cleves and Catherine Howard. She was one of the ladies who gave evidence enabling Henry VIII to annul his marriage to Anne of Cleves and she was executed as a traitor for her part in helping Catherine of Howard have an affair with Thomas Culpeper. Both Culpeper and Catherine blamed her for encouraging them. She was executed on the 13th February 1542.

Nan Cobham

In 1536, Sir John Hussee wrote to Lady Lisle regarding Anne Boleyn's fall, naming a "Nan Cobham" as one of Anne Boleyn's main accusers: "The first accuser, the lady Worcester, and Nan Cobham with one maid mo[re]; but the lady Worcester was the first ground ".[6] But who was he referring to?

Historical novelist Kate Emerson[7], who has done meticulous research into ladies-in-waiting in the Tudor era, writes of how the editor of The Lisle Letters, M. St Clare Byrne, points out that it is very unlikely that Hussee would refer to Baroness Cobham, wife of Sir George Brooke, 9th Baron Cobham, as "Nan Cobham". So what are the possibilities?

- Anne Bray, Baroness Cobham – This Anne Cobham was an attendant horsewoman at Anne Boleyn's coronation on the 1st June 1533 and was married to Thomas Wyatt's brother-in-law, Sir George Brooke. They lived at Cobham Hall in Kent and had ten children. Anne died on 1st November 1558

- The Anne Cobham who served as a lady-in-waiting to Catherine Parr in 1547.

- The widow Anne Cobham who was granted lands in 1540 which used to belong to Syon Abbey.[8]

- The Anne Cobham who was married to Sir Edward Borough, 2nd Baron Borough of Gainsborough, although it is thought that she died in the late 1520s.

- Anne Boleyn's midwife – Retha Warnicke[9] names Nan Cobham as one of the Queen's midwives and also states that the diminutive "Nan" just would not be used for a woman of "high aristocratic birth". Baroness Cobham was the daughter of Sir Edmund Bray(e) who became Baron Bray in 1529 so she was a noblewoman.

Mary Scrope, Lady Kingston

Mary Scrope was the second wife of Sir William Kingston, Constable of the Tower of London and it was also her second marriage. She was appointed to serve Anne Boleyn in May 1536 during her imprisonment in the Tower of London and Mary's job was to report back to her husband on what Anne said so that he could pass the information on to Thomas Cromwell.

Lady Anne Shelton (Anne Boleyn)

Lady Anne Shelton (née Boleyn) was the sister of Thomas Boleyn and therefore Queen Anne Boleyn's aunt. She was married to Sir John Shelton and the couple were in charge of the combined household of Henry VIII's daughters, Mary and Elizabeth, from 1533, with Sir John acting as steward. The couple had nine children, including Margaret and Mary Shelton.

In May 1536, Lady Anne was appointed to serve her niece, Anne Boleyn, during her imprisonment in the Tower. It is thought that Lady Anne did not sympathise with her niece at this point because she had been angry with Anne when she had pushed Mary

Shelton into having an affair with Henry VIII to prevent him from having an affair with a lady not sympathetic to Anne.

Margaret Dymoke (Coffin)

Margaret was born around 1500 and her second husband was Sir William Coffin who was Anne Boleyn's Master of the Horse. Like Lady Anne Shelton and Mary Scrope, Margaret was appointed to serve Anne Boleyn in the Tower in May 1536. After Anne's execution, Margaret went on to become a lady-in-waiting to Jane Seymour.

Lady Elizabeth Boleyn (née Wood)

Lady Boleyn was the wife of Sir James Boleyn, brother of Thomas Boleyn and chancellor of the household of Queen Anne Boleyn. She was, therefore, aunt to Anne Boleyn. She was also one of the women appointed to serve Anne Boleyn in May 1536 in the Tower of London and she, along with Lady Kingston, accompanied Anne Boleyn to her trial on the 15th May 1536.

Elizabeth Stoner (Mrs Stoner)

Elizabeth Stoner was the fifth woman appointed to serve Anne Boleyn in the Tower in order that Anne's words could be reported back to Thomas Cromwell and used as evidence against her. She served under each of Henry VIII's six wives and held the position of 'Mother of the Maids', meaning that she was in charge of the younger ladies-in-waiting.

Jane Seymour

Before becoming Queen, Jane served as a lady-in-waiting, or maid-of-honour, to Queen Catherine of Aragon and Queen Anne Boleyn. She married Henry VIII on the 30th May, just 11 days after the execution of his previous wife, Anne Boleyn, and was the mother of King Edward VI, Henry VIII's only surviving son. She died on the 24th October 1537 probably from puerperal fever (childbed fever), a bacterial infection common after childbirth.

Lady Bridget Wingfield
(née Wiltshire, later Hervey, then Tyrwhitt)

Lady Wingfield was born Bridget Wiltshire and was the daughter of Sir John Wiltshire of Stone Castle, Kent, who was a neighbour of the Boleyn family who lived at Hever Castle. It is thought that she served Catherine of Aragon as a lady-in-waiting and then served Anne as Lady of the Bedchamber. She was married three times: Lord Deputy of Calais Sir Richard Wingfield (d. 1525) in 1513, diplomat Sir Nicholas Hervey/Harvey (d. 1532) and Sir Robert Tyrwhitt.

In "The Rise and Fall of Anne Boleyn", Retha Warnicke,[10] writes of how, in 1530, one of Anne Boleyn's closest companions was Lady Wingfield and that in autumn 1532 Anne and Henry VIII stopped at the home of Lady Wingfield on their way to Dover to travel to France.

Lady Wingfield died in 1533/1534, but her correspondence was used by the Crown in May 1536.[11] It was alleged that Lady Wingfield had written to a friend regarding Anne Boleyn's sex life before she became queen and, according to Retha Warnicke, this made the charges of adultery more believable.[12]

Mary Shelton

Mary was the daughter of Sir John Shelton and Lady Anne Shelton (née Boleyn) and cousin of Anne Boleyn. It is unclear whether she or Margaret Shelton had an affair with Henry VIII but it is now thought that Mary Shelton was the 'Madge Shelton' who Sir Henry Norris was meant to marry and who became the King's mistress. Queen Anne Boleyn allegedly reprimanded Mary for writing 'ydill poesies' in her prayer book.

Mary was due to marry Thomas Clere, a close friend of Henry Howard, Earl of Surrey, but he died in 1545 and Mary went on to marry Sir Anthony Heveningham. The couple had nine children.

Heveningham died in 1557 and Mary married Philip Appleyard. She died in 1571.

Elizabeth Somerset/Elizabeth Browne, Countess of Worcester

Elizabeth Browne was the daughter of Sir Anthony Browne, wife of Henry Somerset, 2nd Earl of Worcester, from c1527, and a lady-in-waiting to Queen Anne Boleyn. She stood to the left of Anne Boleyn at her coronation dinner in 1533 holding a special cloth which would hide the Queen's face when she needed to spit.[13]

It is alleged that she was a mistress of King Henry VIII, and that when her brother, also called Sir Anthony Browne, reprimanded her for her immoral behaviour in 1536, Elizabeth told him that she was "no worse than the queen". This story comes from a poem by Lancelot de Carles[14] and de Carles also has the woman thought to be the Countess of Worcester telling her brother that George Boleyn had carnal knowledge of the Queen. G W Bernard writes of how evidence shows that it was this information which sparked off the arrests in April and May 1536.[15] Anne Boleyn, however, was unaware of this and actually spoke, during her imprisonment in the Tower, of her concern for the Countess and her unborn child: "[Anne] myche lamented my lady of Worceter, for by cause that her child did not store in hyre body. And my wyf sayd, what shuld be the cause? And she said, for the sorow she toke for me."[16]

Trivia: Elizabeth borrowed £100 from Anne Boleyn in April 1536.

Elizabeth Harleston

According to Alan Bryson's article on soldier and diplomat Sir John Wallop,[17] Elizabeth was the daughter of Sir Clement Harleston of South Ockendon, Essex. She married Wallop as his second wife in 1530 and had previously been in Anne Boleyn's service. She also served Anne as an attendant when she and Henry VIII visited

Calais in autumn 1532 to meet Francis I. Kate Emerson[18] writes of how Wallop was a supporter of Catherine of Aragon during the King's Great Matter and Elizabeth was described as a "creatura"[19] (creature) of Catherine's in December 1535, so obviously swapped sides.

Elizabeth was one of the ladies in Jane Seymour's funeral procession in 1536 and she died in March 1552.

Anne Savage

Anne Savage, daughter of Sir John Savage of the Savage family of Clifton, Cheshire, and his wife Anne Bostock, served Anne Boleyn before she was queen and is rumoured to have been one of Anne Boleyn's attendants at her secret marriage to Henry VIII on the 25th January 1533, along with Henry Norris and Thomas Heneage.

Anne married Thomas Berkeley, 6th Baron Berkeley, in April 1533 and the couple lived in Berkeley Castle in Gloucestershire. Berkeley was one of the noblemen made a Knight of the Bath at Anne Boleyn's coronation in the summer of 1533. The couple had two children: a daughter Elizabeth and a son Thomas, 7th Baron Berkeley.

After Berkeley's death in September 1534, Anne had an offer of marriage from Edward Sutton but she refused and never took a second husband.

Margaret Douglas

Lady Margaret Douglas was the daughter of Margaret Tudor, Queen of Scotland, and her second husband Archibald Douglas, 6th Earl of Angus. She was, therefore, King Henry VIII's niece. Margaret joined Anne Boleyn's household after her marriage to Henry VIII and it was there that she fell in love with the Queen's uncle, Lord Thomas Howard. Their relationship caused a scandal when Henry VIII found out in the summer of 1536 and the couple were imprisoned in the Tower. Margaret was then moved to Syon

Abbey. Howard died in the Tower in October 1537 but Margaret was released from Syon shortly before his death.

Margaret was restored to favour in 1537 and went on to serve Anne of Cleves and Catherine Howard. Unfortunately, she was involved in scandal again when she fell in love with Catherine Howard's brother, Charles, and this led to her being sent to Syon and then Kenninghall. She was back in favour by 1543 when she was a bridesmaid at Henry VIII's marriage to Catherine Parr, a queen she went on to serve. On 6th July 1544 she married Matthew Stewart, 13th or 14th Earl of Lennox. The couple's first son died in infancy but her second son survived. He was Henry Stewart, Lord Darnley, the second husband of Mary Queen of Scots. He was murdered in February 1567. Margaret had eight children.

Margaret was put under house arrest in 1561 after she had boasted that her son would marry Mary Queen of Scots and that they would claim the English throne. She was back at court by July 1564 but was sent to the Tower of London in 1565 after the Scottish queen announced her betrothal to Darnley. Margaret was released in 1567.

Lennox was shot at Stirling Castle in 1571 and Margaret was heartbroken. She was imprisoned in the Tower briefly in 1574 and after her release went to live with her son Charles, Earl of Lennox, his wife and daughter Arabella (Arbella). Charles died of tuberculosis in 1576 and Margaret tried, without success, to claim the earldom of Lennox for Arabella. Margaret died on 9th March 1578 after being taken ill after having Robert Dudley, Earl of Leicester, round for supper.[20]

Mary Howard

Mary Howard was the daughter of Thomas Howard, 3rd Duke of Norfolk, and Elizabeth Stafford, and so was cousin to Anne Boleyn. She married Henry VIII's illegitimate son, Henry Fitzroy, Duke of Richmond, in November 1533, but they never lived as man and wife, due to his death in 1536, and the marriage was probably not consummated.

Mary played roles in the ceremony making Anne Boleyn Marquis of Pembroke in 1532 and also in Princess Elizabeth's christening in 1533, and served Anne as a maid of honour.

After her husband's death, she divided her time between Kenninghall in Norfolk and court, where she was a member of the literary circle which included her brother, Henry Howard, Earl of Surrey, and the King's niece, Lady Margaret Douglas. She served Queen Catherine Howard until her arrest in late 1541.

Thomas Seymour, brother of Jane Seymour, was put forward as a potential second husband for Mary but both Mary and her brother were opposed to the idea and the marriage did not go ahead. Mary never remarried.

She was called upon to give evidence against her father and brother in their downfall in 1546 and her brother was executed in January 1547. Fortunately, her father was saved when Henry VIII died before his scheduled execution. Surrey's children became her wards and she appointed John Foxe, the renowned reformer and future martyrologist, to tutor Surrey's three eldest children: Thomas, Jane and Henry.

Mary died around 1555 and was buried with her husband in a tomb at St Michael's Church, Framlingham.

Other Women

Other women who, according to Kate Emerson, made up Anne Boleyn's household between 1533 and 1536 include Mrs Marshall (named as Mistress of the Maidens), Jane Ashley, Mary Norris, Mary Boleyn (Anne's sister), Elizabeth Isley, Grace Newport (Jane Boleyn's sister-in-law), Eleanor Paston (Countess of Rutland), Margaret Stanley (Countess of Suffolk), Frances de Vere (Countess of Surrey), Mary Orchard (a chamberer who used to be Anne Boleyn's nurse) and the silkwomen Joan North and Elizabeth Philip.[21]

Notes and Sources

1. The Life and Death of Anne Boleyn, Eric Ives, p81-82

2. Ibid., p145

3. The Life of Anne Boleigne, George Wyatt,

4. LP vi.1164

5. Eric Ives, p332

6. LP x. 953

7. A Who's Who of Tudor Women, Kate Emerson

8. LP xv.733

9. The Rise and Fall of Anne Boleyn, Retha Warnicke, p203, 209

10. Ibid., 117

11. Ibid., p39

12. Ibid., p227

13. Ibid., p228

14. Lancelot de Carles in L'Opinion, G. Ascoli

15. Anne Boleyn: Fatal Attractions, G W Bernard, p153

16. LP x. 793

17. 'Wallop, Sir John (b. before 1492, d. 1551)', Alan Bryson, Oxford Dictionary of National Biography, Oxford University Press, 2004

18. A Who's Who of Tudor Women, Kate Emerson

19. LP ix. 970

20. 'Douglas, Lady Margaret, countess of Lennox (1515–1578)', Rosalind K Marshall, Oxford Dictionary of National Biography, Oxford University Press, 2004

21. Anne Boleyn's Household, Lists of Women at Court, http://www.kateemersonhistoricals.com

Anne Boleyn's Household

In the previous article, I discussed some of the female members of Anne Boleyn's household, the women who served her as ladies-in-waiting, but they were not the only members of the household. There were also positions concerned with administration, staffing, money and religion, and these posts were held by men.

Here are a few of the men who worked for Anne...

William Coffin – Master of the Horse

William Coffin was born around 1495, joined King Henry VIII's privy chamber in 1515 and was the King's Master of the Horse at the Field of the Cloth of Gold in 1520. He was Anne Boleyn's Master of the Horse at her coronation in 1533, where he was knighted.

Eric Ives, in "The Life and Death of Anne Boleyn", describes William Coffin as Anne's "household administrator and explains that he was in charge of staffing issues.[1] He went on to serve Jane Seymour in the same position and his wife, Margaret Dymoke, was appointed to serve Anne Boleyn in the Tower and to report back to Sir William Kingston everything that Anne said while imprisoned.

He died in 1538.

George Taylor – Receiver General

George Taylor was a part of Anne Boleyn's household before she became queen and Ives believes he may have begun his royal career as a lawyer. He was paid a salary of £50, a large amount, so his job was an important one.[2]

According to Wikipedia, "Receiver General" is an alternative name for the post of "treasurer", i.e. someone responsible for making and receiving payments on behalf of an institution.

Thomas Cromwell – High Steward

Letters and Papers[3] lists Thomas Cromwell being paid £20 for being "High Steward of the Queen's Lands" in September 1535 and Eric Ives writes of how it was he who sent Anne the warrant for the delivery of her letters patent giving her the title of Marquis of Pembroke. He was also probably involved in directing the survey of her lands in Wales[4]. It was also Cromwell who organised Anne's coronation in 1533.

Although Cromwell was Anne Boleyn's high steward, he was only involved in "major policy issues"[5] which concerned the Queen, rather than the trivial day-to-day business. When Anne was on the rise in the early 1530s, Cromwell was definitely Anne's man, a man she could rely on, but he also served her husband, Henry VIII, as his official chief minister and secretary from April 1534. His relationship with the King was obviously his priority and when he saw that Anne was threatening this he conspired against her and her circle. There is controversy regarding his exact role in Anne Boleyn's downfall and whether it was his idea, or that of the King, but he took full credit for the plot when he discussed it with Eustace Chapuys, the imperial ambassador. Anne Boleyn, her brother and four other men were executed in May 1536 after being found guilty of treason and adultery.

James Boleyn – Chancellor

Sir James Boleyn was Anne's uncle, being the younger brother of her father, Thomas Boleyn, and he was a man who shared her religious beliefs. Anne appointed him as her chancellor but she was not close to his wife, Lady Elizabeth Boleyn (née Wood). Lady Boleyn was one of the five women appointed to serve Anne in the Tower and accompanied Anne to her trial on the 15th May 1536 with Lady Kingston.

Thomas, Lord Burgh (Borough) of Gainsborough – Lord Chamberlain

Thomas Burgh was born in Gainsborough, Lincolnshire, in around 1488 and was the son of Edward Burgh, 2nd Baron Burgh, and Anne Cobham, 6th Baroness Cobham. He was knighted in 1513 at the Battle of Flodden Field and held the post of Sheriff of Lincolnshire in 1518-19 and 1524-25. He was summoned to the House of Lords in 1529 as Lord Burgh after his father became mentally ill.

Anne Boleyn appointed him as her Lord Chamberlain and one of the first things he did was rip Catherine of Aragon's badge from her barge and seize it for the new queen.[6] He rode in Anne's barge in her coronation procession and also held her train in her coronation ceremony. In 1536, "Thos. Lord Burgh"[7] was named as one of the jury at Anne Boleyn's trial so he was one of the men who found his former mistress guilty of treason and adultery.

His son, Sir Edward Burgh (Borough) was the first husband of Catherine Parr, Henry VIII's sixth and final wife.

Sir Edward Baynton – Vice Chamberlain

Sir Edward Baynton (Bayntun) was born around 1480 at Faulston House, Faulston, Wiltshire, and he inherited the manors of Faulston and Bromham on his father's death in 1516. He was said to have been friends with, and to have possibly served, Queen Catherine of Aragon, who funded the reconstruction of the gates of his manor in Bromham. He was a favourite of Henry VIII, who granted him large areas of land in Wiltshire, and served Anne Boleyn as Vice Chamberlain from 1533. His home, Bromham House, was one of the properties Anne and Henry visited on their famous royal progress in the summer of 1535.

Eric Ives writes of how he shared some of Anne's religious beliefs, but this did not stop him from being involved in trying to obtain confessions from the men alleged to have had affairs with Anne Boleyn.

After Anne Boleyn's fall in May 1536, he was appointed Jane Seymour's Master of the Horses and then went on to serve Henry VIII's subsequent wives as vice chamberlain. His wife, Isabel (née Legh), was Catherine Howard's half-sister and served Catherine as one of her ladies after her marriage to Henry VIII in 1540.

Edward Baynton was also a soldier and he died on the 27th November 1544 of wounds sustained in battle.

John Uvedale (Udall) – Secretary

Uvedale began his career during the reign of Henry VII, serving the King as an exchequer clerk, and rose to be the treasurer for the northern garrisons during the reign of Edward VI.[8] While serving Anne Boleyn as secretary, he also served as secretary to Henry VIII's illegitimate son, Henry Fitzroy, Duke of Richmond.

John Smith – Surveyor

John Smith was a "professional auditor"[9] who went on to serve Anne's successor, Jane Seymour.

Henry Cryche

Henry Cryche was Anne Boleyn's clerk of the wardrobe.

William Lock

William Lock (Lok) was Anne's mercer. and he was also involved in travelling to the Low Countries to bring back reformist literature for the Queen.

Receivers

One of Anne's receivers was John Poinz,[10] brother, of Thomas Poinz. Thomas Poinz was the landlord of William Tyndale, the Bible translator, in Antwerp in 1535 when Tyndale was arrested.

Others

Eric Ives explains that if Anne Boleyn's council was like that of Catherine of Aragon, then it would consist of a chancellor (James Boleyn), receiver general (Tayor), surveyor (Smith) and also an auditor, attorney-general, solicitor-general, clerk, six lawyers and three court attorney.[11]

Chaplains

William Latymer, Hugh Latimer, William Betts and Matthew Parker were all men who served Anne Boleyn as her personal chaplains.

Dr William Butts, Henry VIII's physician, acted as Anne Boleyn's "talent spotter",[12] helping Anne to choose her chaplains from scholars at Cambridge, those with reformist sympathies, particularly Butts' old college, Gonville Hall. It was Butts who introduced Hugh Latimer to Anne.

Hugh Latimer

Hugh Latimer was born around between 1480 and 1494 in Thurcaston, Lancashire. He studied at the University of Cambridge and worked there as the university preacher and chaplain. He was deeply affected by hearing the confession of Thomas Bilney, a man who was later burned for heresy in 1531, and began to accept reformed doctrines, meeting regularly with the likes of Bilney and Robert Barnes, who was also burned for heresy. Latimer was appointed as Bishop of Worcester in 1535, an appointment which is said to have been due to the patronage of Anne Boleyn who was queen at this time.

Latimer was imprisoned in the Tower of London in 1539 for his opposition to Henry VIII's Six Articles but was restored to favour during the reign of Edward VI, becoming a court preacher and chaplain to Catherine Willoughby, the Duchess of Suffolk. Latimer was burned at the stake with Nicholas Ridley on the 16th October 1555 in Oxford, during the reign of the Catholic queen,

Mary I.

Matthew Parker

Matthew Parker was born on the 6th August 1504 in Norwich and was educated at Corpus Christi College in Cambridge, where he became friends with a group of reformers. He was appointed chaplain to Henry VIII in 1537 and also served as Anne Boleyn's chaplain. It was Anne's patronage which led to him being appointed dean of the collegiate church of Stoke by Clare in Suffolk.[13]

On the 26th April 1536, Anne Boleyn asked Parker to ensure that her daughter, Elizabeth, was looked after if anything should happen to Anne. On the 19th May 1536, just under a month after Anne had spoken to Parker, Anne was executed. Parker kept his word and he was rewarded for his loyalty by Elizabeth I in 1559 when she appointed him as her Archbishop of Canterbury. He died on the 17th May 1575.

Matthew Parker is also known for being one of the men responsible for the Thirty-Nine Articles of Religion which were established in 1563 and which are seen as "the historic defining statements of Anglican doctrine in relation to the controversies of the English Reformation".[14]

William Betts

It is not known when William Betts was born but he studied at both Gonville Hall and Corpus Christi College at the University of Cambridge before becoming Anne's chaplain.

In 1528, Betts had been involved in scandal at Oxford, with the likes of Matthew Parker, Hugh Latimer and Thomas Garret, concerning the circulation of prohibited religious books. Garret went on to be burned at the stake for heresy in 1540. It was Betts who recommended Matthew Parker to Anne, and Parker replaced Betts as Anne's chaplain in 1535 after Betts' death.

John Skip (Skypp) – Almoner

John Skip studied at Gonville Hall, Cambridge University, graduating in 1518. His career included being vicar of the parishes of Newington and Shepway, being Anne Boleyn's almoner when she was queen, being the Archdeacon of Suffolk from 1536-1539 and being Bishop of Hereford from 1539-1552.

On Passion Sunday 1536, John Skip preached a sermon which caused controversy.[15] Although he defended the rituals and ceremonies of the church as aids to memory, he attacked the king's counsel, the English clergy and the Crown's greed. Skip referred to King Solomon who, later in his reign, "defamed himself"[16] by giving in to lust, by taking multiple wives and concubines, and avarice.

As Eric Ives explains, Skip then went on discuss the story of Esther and it was clear that he saw Anne Boleyn as Esther, Henry VIII as Ahasuerus, Cromwell as Haman and the clergy as the Jews in the story.[17] He was attacking the King's counsellors for the advice they were giving the King which was based on greed and personal gain, so he was therefore attacking Thomas Cromwell, the King's minister. Anne had fallen out with Cromwell over the proceeds of the dissolution of the monasteries, which she pointed out were going to the Crown rather than into supporting educational and charitable causes. As Anne's almoner, he was preaching what Anne wanted him to preach.

On the night of the 17th/18th May 1536, the night before Anne Boleyn believed that she was going to be executed, John Skip visited her at 2am to pray with her. At dawn on the 19th May, the day Anne was actually executed, she celebrated the mass and received the sacrament from Skip. She was executed by the sword that morning.

Notes and Sources

1. The Life and Death of Anne Boleyn, Eric Ives, p211
2. Ibid.
3. LP ix.478
4. Ives, p207
5. Ibid., p211
6. Ibid.
7. LP x.876
8. Ives, p211
9. Ibid, p263
10. Ibid.p211
11. Ibid
12. Ibid., p266
13. Ibid
14. Wikipedia – Article on the Thirty-Nine Articles
15. Ives, p307
16. Ibid., p308
17. Ibid.

The Lost Boleyns – Thomas and Henry Boleyn

In her book "Mary Boleyn: The Great and Infamous Whore", Alison Weir claims that Thomas Boleyn the Younger, brother of Anne Boleyn, lived into adulthood and died in 1520. Weir based her conclusion on the following evidence:-

- Thomas's tomb is marked with the date 1520.

- He was named after his father and grandfather and therefore must have been the eldest son

Now, I was very puzzled about this conclusion as I have always believed that Thomas's tomb at Penshurst was that of an infant, just like his brother Henry Boleyn's at St Peter's Church, Hever, which is also a tiny tomb marked by a simple cross. As someone who is researching the Boleyns on a daily basis for The Anne Boleyn Files and my book, I just couldn't let this rest, so, I made it my mission to find out more about these lost Boleyns.

Mission Lost Boleyns

The first step in Mission Lost Boleyns was to get the help of my friend, Clare Cherry, who has written a book on George Boleyn. All of this blew up while I was on The Anne Boleyn Experience in July 2011 and Clare was one of the participants on this tour. Clare and her trusty sidekick, David, had told me that they were visiting Penshurst Place after the tour, so I asked if they would be interested in visiting St John the Baptist Church at Penshurst with Tim (my trusty sidekick) and I, to do some digging. I knew Clare would be excited about this and she agreed, off we went to Penshurst...

In the beautiful village church, just outside Penshurst Place, Clare, David, Tim and I, visited the tomb of little Thomas Boleyn in the Sidney Chapel. It was very moving to see this tiny, and very simple, tomb amongst all the large and lavish tombs of the

Sidney family and to pay our respects to a Boleyn who is often forgotten. After we had paid our respects, Clare and I got down on our hands and knees to examine the brass cross, the inscription and surrounding stone work. What we found was a very simple and plain brass cross inscribed with "Thomas Bwllayen the sone of Sir Thomas Bwllayen". No date, no other information, just that. We took photos and then I turned to the church information table which had a guide book on the church. I purchased it, flicked through it on the spot and read aloud that Thomas was the infant brother of Anne Boleyn and that he had died in 1520.

Hmmm... Clare and I looked at each other "Where did they get that date from?" was the obvious question, so Mission Lost Boleyns continued with the following investigations being undertaken:-

- Email to Alison Weir – Ask her what she bases the 1520 death date on as the tomb is not marked with a date

- Contact author of the church guide book re 1520 death date

- Research Parish Records for Thomas Boleyn's death date

Results of Initial Investigations

- Alison Weir – Alison Weir emailed me straight back explaining that an Ashmolean Museum record gave the same date for the brass as the church leaflet. I then did some digging in the Ashmolean Museum's online records of monumental brasses and found that Henry Boleyn's brass cross was also dated 1520. I emailed Weir back saying that I wondered if the records referred to the date that the brasses were actually made and put on the tomb, rather than the date of death. Weir replied that she felt that Henry Boleyn's tomb was that of an infant due to its "tiny" size.

- David Lough, author of the Guide Book – Clare managed to track down David Lough, author of the church guide book, to ask about the 1520 date and he explained that the current guide book was based on an older guide book and he could not remember where the 1520 date came from but that "there are arguments for thinking it might have been 1521. In that year [actually 1522], Sir Tomas Bwllayen was appointed Keeper of Penshurst Place by Henry VIII following the property's reversion to the Crown after the execution for treason of its previous owner, the Duke of Buckingham. According to 'Penshurst Church: the Hidden History', J.A Flower (private paper, 2004), It seems likely that the infant Thomas fell ill during one of his father's visits as Keeper, to Penshurst Place from his own nearby Hever Castle." He admitted that Clare probably knew far more about the Boleyns than he did!

- Parish Records – Unfortunately, Clare found that these only went back as far as c.1558, so they were not any help.

All this was very interesting but it left us with more questions rather than answers! I was puzzled that Alison Weir was claiming that Thomas Boleyn the Younger's tomb was that of an adult yet saying that Henry Boleyn's at Hever, which was identical in size and design, was that of an infant. On the other hand, Clare and I were also both bemused by the idea that Elizabeth Boleyn was still producing babies c1520 at the age of around 40, old by Tudor standards. None of it made sense. More digging was required.

I went back to the Ashmolean records and used their bibliography and list of sources for monumental brasses to find records of Thomas Boleyn the Younger's brass. In "A List of Monumental Brasses in the British Isles" by Mill Stephenson (1926), which was based on older, 19th century records, I found the following:-

- Penshurst – "Sm. cross (partly restored) and inscr. to Thos., son of Sir Thos. Bwllayen, c.1520"

- Hever – "Sm. cross (restored) and inscr. to Hen., son of Sir Thos. Bwllayen, c.1520. At Penshurst is a similar memorial to Thos., another son of Sir Thos. Bullen."

In another book, W D Belcher's "Kentish Brasses" Vol I (1888), it said of the Penshurst brass: "Small cross with inscription for Thomas Bullayen, son of Sir Thomas Bullen" and had a drawing of the brass cross and inscription.

So, c.1520 was the date given to both brass crosses, at Hever and Penshurst. Surely the boys didn't die in the same year? This made us wonder if the brass crosses were placed on the tombs at a later date, perhaps when the family had the means and inclination to mark these tombs in a fitting manner. In times when infant mortality was very high, it would not have been unusual, I feel, for these tombs to have been unmarked for a few years.

After all this digging, Mission Lost Boleyns seemed to come to a standstill. Clare and I concluded that the size and style of the tombs suggested that Thomas and Henry Boleyn were indeed infants and that the "c.1520" date was the date of the brasses rather than the date of the death. The fact that Thomas Boleyn the Younger was buried at Penshurst, rather than Hever, had been bothering us but Clare wondered if the renovation work that Thomas Boleyn carried out on Hever, after he inherited it in 1505, forced the family to stay with their friend and relative the Duke of Buckingham at nearby Penshurst. Perhaps little Thomas died while they were staying there, we just don't know.

After I contacted Alison Weir, she also made some investigations and explained on her website that her dating of Thomas's tomb and death was based on three sources:-

- John Flower's book on Penshurst village - He dated the brass cross and tomb to 1520

- The Penshurst Church leaflet, which also gave 1520 as the date.

- The Ashmolean Museum website's list of monumental brasses which corroborated the date.

Weir then explained that she had been alerted by a reader (me) that the tomb actually did not have a date inscribed on it so she decided to do further research. She asked the vicar of Penhurst to check the brass and to let her know where the dating came from. He explained to her that the late John Flower, archivist, had concluded that little Thomas was born at Penshurst after his father had become Keeper of Penhurst. Weir rightly dismissed that line of argument because Thomas Boleyn did not become Keeper until 1522.

Interestingly, Weir then concluded that the brass must date after June 1509 because it describes Thomas Boleyn the Younger as son of "Sir" Thomas Boleyn and Thomas Boleyn the Elder was not knighted until June 1509. She then went on to say that she felt that the size of the brass did not necessarily mean that Thomas Boleyn was an infant when he died. Weir wrote of how she believed him to have been the eldest son and possibly the one who attended Oxford. She also put forward the idea that he may have been born in the mid to late 1490s and that after university he joined the Duke of Buckingham's household at Penshurst.

Weir also stated that she contacted the Ashmolean Museum to find out their source for the date and that Dr Eleanor Standley, Lecturer and Assistant Keeper of Medieval Archaeology, Institute of Archaeology/ Department of Antiquities, Ashmolean Museum, University of Oxford, explained that she thought the brass had been dated to c.1520 on stylistic grounds. She also pointed out that Macklin's Monumental Brasses (1969) gave the date as c.1520. As for Henry Boleyn, Weir commented that his cross was also dated to 1520 and that he also may have lived into early adulthood, possibly dying around the same time.

I disagree with Weir's theory in her book and the statements on her website because:-

- Weir came out with a controversial and ground-breaking theory, i.e. that Thomas Boleyn the Younger died as an adult in 1520, in a book, citing evidence that is now proven to be suspect. The tomb is NOT marked 1520 and no sources seem to be able to explain the c.1520 dating of the cross.

- Weir has changed her mind about the relevance of the size of the tombs.

- Her justification of the 1520 death date for an adult Thomas

Boleyn – That he was born in the mid to late 1490s and that after studying at Oxford he may have entered the household of the Duke of Buckingham. She does use the words "likely ", "if" and "possible", but this is pure supposition. It is believed that Elizabeth and Thomas Boleyn married 1498/1499, and not before. Eric Ives believes that Elizabeth Howard's jointure, which was settled on her in mid 1501, suggests that the Boleyns had been married fairly recently and so not before 1498. He goes on to suggest that Mary was born c1499, Anne in 1501 and George c1504. I believe that Thomas and Henry Boleyn were born between Anne and George, or Thomas possibly between Mary and Anne. As for the whole Oxford issue, it is tradition that George Boleyn attended Oxford University, but there are no records to confirm his attendance there or that of another Boleyn sibling. What I do know, from my research into the Boleyns, is that Thomas Boleyn the Younger is not mentioned in the records and surely, as the son of a rising star at court, he'd be mentioned if he hadn't died in infancy. There is a "Master Bollyn" recorded as taking part in the Christmas festivities of 1514 with his father, Sir Thomas Boleyn, but this is thought to refer to George and it is only George who is mentioned in later records. Surely a son born in the mid to late 1490s who joined the Duke of Buckingham's household would be mentioned?

• The 1509 Sir Thomas Boleyn argument – Weir argues that the tombs must date to after 1509 because the inscriptions refer to "Sir" Thomas Boleyn as their father. This can be explained by the brasses being placed on the tombs later, it does not mean that the boys died after 1509 or that they lived until 1520.

These lost Boleyns are still lost, in that they are still a mystery in my eyes. There is no date on their tombs, they are not named in any records or contemporary sources, the date given in records of monumental brasses is CIRCA 1520 and also refers to the brasses not the tombs. The trail has gone dead for the time being. We can have opinions about these boys but they are just that, opinions. I will carry on believing that those simple, tiny tombs at Hever and Penshurst belong to the little Boleyns who died young but fortunately escaped being brought down so brutally with their sister and brother in 1536.

RIP Thomas and Henry Boleyn, the lost Boleyns.

Notes and Sources

- "THOMAS BULLAYEN" – BRASS IN THE SIDNEY CHAPEL, PENSHURST CHURCH, on Alison Weir's website alisonweir.org.uk/books/bookpages/more-mary-boleyn.asp

- The Life and Death of Anne Boleyn, Eric Ives, p10, 14 and 17

- LP ii. REVEL ACCOUNTS NO.7

- The brains and research of Clare Cherry and Claire Ridgway, with the support of David and Tim!

- 2011 Guide and History, Church of St John the Baptist, Penshurst, by David Lough

- The Department of Antiquities: Monumental Brasses, Ashmolean Museum

- A List of Monumental Brasses in the British Isles (1926) by Mill Stephenson

- Kentish Brasses by W D Belcher (1888)

- Mary Boleyn: The Mistress of Kings by Alison Weir, p12 and 19

- The Other Boleyn Boy – Did a Fourth Boleyn Sibling Survive to Maturity?, Natalie Grueninger from the On the Tudor Trail blog

The Lost Boleyns –
Update on the Tomb Brasses
of Thomas and Henry Boleyn

Further to my investigations into the monumental brass crosses on the tombs of Thomas and Henry Boleyn, brothers of Anne Boleyn, I have just had an answer back from Michael Harris of the Monumental Brass Society. Michael spoke to the Society's Kentish expert who said:-

"The Bullen crosses are two "one-offs" of the same design. There was a small workshop in Kent around 1500-1530/35 which produced some rather low quality brasses with a very debased script style. Most of them are listed by Mill Stephenson as "local". The design was never a style, just a bit of Kentish localism. The earlier cross brasses of the fourteenth century in particular were of course high quality, mainly London work for priests. The Bullen examples are almost certainly to children."

I checked my copy of Mill Stephenson's "A List of Monumental Brasses in the British Isles" and it does indeed say "local" in its records of the two brasses:-

"Sm. cross (partly restored) and inscr. to Thos., son of Sir Thos. Bwllayen, c.1520, local, S.C [South Chapel]" – Penshurst

"Sm. cross (restored) and inscr. to Hen., son of Sir Thos. Bwllayen, c.1520, local, N.C. [North Chapel]" – Hever

So, the Monumental Brass Society, who are experts on brasses, date these brass crosses to 1500-1535 and believe that they mark the tombs of children. I guess that "c.1520" was a good date for the Ashmolean and other records to pick as it's pretty much in the middle of this period, but it certainly does not mean that those two boys died in 1520. In the absence of evidence to back up the 1520 date (and therefore to back up Alison Weir's theory that Thomas, and possibly Henry, were adults when they died) and in light of the fact that the style of brasses and tomb suggest children's tombs, I believe that these boys died in infancy or early childhood in the early 1500s. Of course, that is my opinion and I cannot say for certain.

Source

- Monumental Brass Society
- A List of Monumental Brasses in the British Isles (1926) by Mill Stephenson

The Lost Boleyns – Claire's still digging!

I am still on the trail of the lost Boleyns, the boys Thomas and Henry thought to have died in infancy or childhood, so don't worry, I'm like a dog with a bone! But while I was doing some research on the Boleyn family this weekend, trying to find sources for what authors write about them, I stumbled upon a fascinating section on Elizabeth Boleyn, Countess of Wiltshire's Wikipedia page which explained how Thomas and Elizabeth had seven children:-

- Mary Boleyn, mistress of Henry VIII of England (c. 1499 – 19 July 1543).
- Henry Boleyn – thought to have died young. (1500–1501)
- Anne Boleyn, queen consort of Henry VIII of England (c. 1501 – 19 May 1536)
- William Boleyn – thought to have died young. (1502–1503)
- Margaret Boleyn – thought to have died young. (1503–1504)
- George Boleyn, Viscount Rochford (c. 1504 – 17 May 1536).
- Catherine Boleyn – thought to have died young. (1505–1506)"

Enlightening, don't you think? Can you hear the sarcasm in my voice? It did make me chuckle because the only children we have hard evidence for are Mary, Anne, George, Henry and Thomas the Younger, yet Thomas doesn't even make it to this list! Instead, we have William, Margaret and Catherine.

Now, I believe that there are bound to have been more Boleyn children that did not survive childhood or that were stillborn, but quite where the author of this Wiki page got this information from I just don't know! Unfortunately, they have not cited any sources or given a reference for this list. Hmmm...

What I did find this weekend was an interesting book on the history of St Peter's Church, Hever, in which the author, John Eastman, Parish Clerk, writes "That there were other brasses in the church at some time was shown in 1894, when several broken pieces were found under the floor." Could it be that there were other Boleyn brasses on the floor of this church in the 16th century? Who knows?

I've also been digging into the records of monumental brasses this weekend (yes, very sad, I know!) and I've been through many, many books on the subject and so far the only brass that I can find that sounds like it is similar in design to the small brass crosses of the Boleyn boys' tombs is one in the Parish Church of North Tuddenham, Norfolk. The record says:-

"Sm. cross bearing an inscr. to Frances, dau. of Thos. Skippe, esq., 1625, aged 2."

So, a 2 year old girl whose tomb is marked by a small brass cross!

Unfortunately there is no rubbing or drawing of it in the records but it sounds exactly like the crosses marking the tombs of Henry and Thomas.

This is the only small brass cross I have found so far and I've been through many hundreds, perhaps even thousands, of brasses now, so this really does make me think that crosses were used on children's tombs. Obviously, it is not conclusive evidence that the Boleyn boys were children when they died, so I am still digging.

Notes and Sources

- Elizabeth Boleyn, Countess of Wiltshire, Wikipedia page
- Historic Hever: The Church, John Eastman, Parish Clerk, 1905
- "A List of Monumental Brasses in the British Isles", Mill Stephenson, 1926

George Boleyn, Lord Rochford, Part 1

Our views and opinions of George Boleyn, Lord Rochford, are often coloured by depictions of him in series like "The Tudors", and movies and books like "The Other Boleyn Girl", but was Anne Boleyn's brother really a bisexual, or even homosexual man, who raped his wife and had affairs with young men? Was he the depraved libertine of Retha Warnicke's "The Rise and Fall of Anne Boleyn" who was linked to sodomy, bestiality and other such "abominable" acts? Did he commit incest with his sister Anne Boleyn to help her provide Henry VIII with an heir to the throne or was he actually something else entirely?

The Boleyn Family

Josephine Wilkinson, author of "The Early Loves of Anne Boleyn", writes of how Anne Boleyn was born in early summer 1500 or 1501, a second daughter to Thomas Boleyn and Elizabeth Howard who already had a daughter, Mary. Thomas and Elizabeth went on to have at least three sons, Henry, Thomas and George, but it was only George who survived childhood. It is generally thought that he was born around 1504, making him around three years younger than Anne.

According to Wilkinson, while his sisters were probably educated together at home, at Hever Castle in Kent, George went to Oxford to be educated before joining the court of Henry VIII to follow in his father's footsteps as a diplomat and courtier. Eric Ives also writes of how George was probably a product of Oxford University and that as well as carrying out diplomatic duties he was also a recognised court poet. Ives writes of how we know that George played in a mummery in the Christmas revels of Christmas 1514-1515, so must have been a child at that time, and then went on to become a royal page.

By 1525 George was married and that by the end of 1529, he

had risen to become a member of the King's privy chamber. There is a remark made by Jean du Bellay in 1529 implying that he thought George was too young to be sent to France as ambassador and, if we take 1504 as his birthdate, 25 may have been seen as rather too young for this type of position, but then George's family was in high favour with the King at this time, the King being besotted with Anne Boleyn.

Career and Life at Court

George Boleyn enjoyed a high profile career at court. Here are some of the positions and grants he was given during his time at court:-

- 1522 – In April 1522 George and his father, Thomas, were given "various offices, in survivorship, in the manor, honor and town of Tunbridge, the manors of Brasted and Pensherst, and the parks of Pensherst, Northlegh and Northlaundes, Kent; with various fees and power to lease" (LP 3. 2214). It has been suggested that this may have been an 18th birthday present for George

- 1524 – In July 1524, according to the Letters and Papers, Foreign and Domestic, Henry VIII, "Geo. Boleyn. Grant of the manor of Grymston, Norfolk, lately held by Sir Thos. Lovell. Westm., 2 July" (LP 3. 2214).

- 1525 – Appointed as a gentleman of the King's privy chamber but lost this position just 6 months later when Wolsey reorganised the King's court and weeded out those he didn't like and trust.

- 1526 – In January 1526, George was appointed as Royal Cupbearer.

- 1528 – A letter from Henry VIII to Anne Boleyn tells us that George contracted sweating sickness while at Waltham Abbey with the King and Catherine of Aragon. In the letters, Henry assures Anne of her brother's recovery, he was one of the lucky ones. Henry writes: "For when we were at Walton, two ushers, two valets de chambres and your brother, master-treasurer, fell ill, but are now quite well. (Love Letters of Henry VIII to Anne Boleyn).

- 1528 – The Letters and Papers record "George Bulleyn, squire of the body" and in the same year he was also made Master of the King's Buckhounds.

- November 1528 – The Letters and Papers record another grant for George Boleyn: "Geo. Bulleyn, squire of the Body. To be keeper of the palace of Beaulieu, alias the manor and mansion of Newhall, Essex; gardener or keeper of the garden and orchard of Newhall; warrener or keeper of the warren in the said manor or lordship; keeper of the wardrobe in the said palace or manor in Newhall, Dorhame, Walkefare Hall and Powers, Essex; with certain daily fees in each office, and the power of leasing the said manor, lands, &c. for his lifetime. Del. Westm., 15 Nov. 20 Hen. VIII" (LP 4. 4993 Grants in November 1528).

- 1st February 1529 – The Letters and Papers record "For GEORGE BULLEYN - To be chief steward of the honor of Beaulieu, Essex, and of all possessions which are annexed by authority of Parliament or otherwise, and keeper of the New Park there, in the manor of Newehall; with 10l. a year for the former, and 3d. a day for the latter; vice William Cary.Del. Westm., 1 Feb. 20 Hen. VIII." (LP 4. 5248). He was later granted a life interest in Beaulieu.

- 27th July 1529 – Another grant is recorded in the Letters and Papers: "27. Geo. Bulleyn, squire of the body. To be governor of the hospital of St. Mary of Bethlem, near Bishopesgate, London. Del. Westm., 27 July 21 Hen. VIII." (LP 4. 5815).

- October 1529 – A letter written by Chapuys to Charles V states how Chapuys was escorted to the King by a gentleman named Poller/Bollen (thought to be Boleyn). (LP 4. 6026)

- December 1529 – In Letters and Papers there is record of

"Instructions to George Boleyn, gentleman of the Privy Chamber, and John Stokesley, D.D., sent to the French king" telling them to consult with Sir Francis Bryan on their arrival at the French Court.(LP iv 6073). The mission of George and Stokesley's diplomatic visits to France were to encourage support for the King's divorce from Catherine of Aragon.

- December 1529 – In the list of peers (LP 4. 6083), it says "Sir Th. Boleyn as visc. Rochford" and then later (LP 4. 6085) "For THOS. VISCOUNT ROCHEFORD, K.G. - Charter, granting, in tail male, the title of earl of Wiltshire in England, with an annuity of 20l. out of the issues of Wilts and Devon; and the title of earl of Ormond in Ireland, with an annuity of 10l. out of the farm of the city of Waterford. (fn. 4) Witnesses: W. archbishop of Canterbury, Thos. duke of Norfolk, treasurer of England, and Chas. duke of Suffolk, marshal of England; Thos. marquis of Dorset, and Hen. marquis of Exeter; John earl of Oxford, chamberlain of England, and Geo. earl of Shrewsbury, steward of the Household; Arthur viscount Lysle, William lord Sands, the King's chamberlain, George lord Bergavenny, Sir William Fitzwilliam, treasurer of the Household, and Sir Henry Guldeford, comptroller of the Household, and others. York Place, 8 Dec. 21 Hen. VIII. Del. Westm., 8 Dec." This made George Boleyn Lord Rochford.

- 5th February 1533 – Letters and Papers record that George Boleyn was summoned to Parliament:"Fiat for writs of summons as follows :—i. Geo. Boleyn, lord Rocheford, to be present in Parliament this Wednesday. Westm., 5 Feb. 24 Hen. VIII." (LP 4. 123) and it is noted that his attendance rate was higher than many others and shows how committed he was to Henry's new Reformation Parliament. He was very influential in parliament and it is also noted that his views on religious reforms and curbing the Pope's powers in England earned him many enemies and that one such man, Lord

LaWarr was on the jury which found him guilty at his trial in May 1536.

- March 1533 – George, Viscount Rochford, was sent to France to present King Francis I with letters from Henry VIII, "written in the King's own hand" informing the French king of his marriage to Anne Boleyn and encouraging his support for this marriage (LP 5. 230). Henry VIII enclosed a letter that he proposed that Francis should write to the Pope, urging him to support the divorce. George was successful in this mission.

- May-August 1533 – George travelled to France again on an embassy with the Duke of Norfolk, his uncle, to be present at a meeting that was supposed to take place between the Pope and Francis I. It was while he was in France that he learned that the Pope had excommunicated Henry so he returned to England to give this news to the King. (LP 6. 556, 692, 918, 954)

- April 1534 – George sent to France again with instructions to encourage Francis I's support for Henry's cause. (LP 7. 470)

- June 1534 – Letters and Papers state: "George lord Rocheford. To be constable of Dover Castle and warden of the Cinque Ports. Del. Westm., 23 June 26 Hen. VIII." (LP 7. 922) These were the highest honours that could be bestowed on a man by the King and George took these appointments very seriously. A letter from George to Cromwell on 26th November 1534 shows George's anger at Cromwell undermining orders that he made as Lord Warden of the Cinque Ports. (LP, 7. 1478)

- July 1534 – George sent to France yet again with instructions to rearrange the meeting between Anne, Henry and Francis I due to Anne's pregnancy and her not wishing to travel in that state. (LP 7. 958)

- May 1535 – George's final diplomatic mission to France. The purpose of this visit was to negotiate a marriage contract between Princess Elizabeth and the third son of the King of

France. (LP 8. 663, 666, 726, 909)

- May 1535 – A letter from Eustace Chapuys in the Calendar of State Papers (Spanish) shows that George, his father and the dukes of Norfolk and Richmond were present at the executions of 3 Carthusian monks who, like Sir Thomas More, had refused to swear allegiance to the Acts of Supremacy and Succession.

- 1st July 1535 – In Letters and Papers, George, Lord Rochford, is named as one of the commissioners at the special sessions of oyer and terminer set up to try Sir Thomas More (LP 8.974).

The numerous mentions of George Boleyn, Lord Rochford, in The Privy Purse Expenses of Henry VIII, show what favour and high regard the King held him in. We know that from these records that George accompanied the King shooting and played bowls, dice, cards and other such games with him.

George, Poetry and Religion

As well as being an influential man at Parliament and having an impressive diplomatic career, George was also a well known and talented court poet, although his poems are now lost or have been attributed to the likes of Thomas Wyatt and Henry Howard. Like his sister, Anne Boleyn, he loved poetry and the arts, was committed to religious reform and was highly intelligent and educated. He translated two evangelical religious texts from French to English for his sister, dedicating them "To the right honourable lady, the Lady Marchioness of Pembroke, her most loving and friendly brother sendeth greetings" and it was George who encouraged Anne to share reformist writings with the King.

Personal Life

George Boleyn married Jane Parker, daughter of Henry Parker, the 10th Baron Morley, and his wife Alice St John, in late 1524/ early 1525. In January 1526, a note in Cardinal Wolsey's hand confirms that "the young Boleyn and his wife" were given the sum of £20 and in 1524 George had been given Grimston Manor in Norfolk, perhaps as a wedding present.

There is much speculation about the Rochford marriage with the traditional view being that the marriage was unhappy. In "The Tudors", we see George's disdain for his wife and Jane's resentment and jealousy of George's relationship with Anne, and this would explain why she allegedly gave evidence against them at their trials, accusing them of incest.

But, is this true? Was it a loveless marriage?

It is hard to say and I don't think we will ever know the truth.

Julia Fox, Jane Parker's biographer, challenges the notion that it was a loveless marriage but Alison Weir believes it was unhappy and that Jane testifying to George having committed incest is evidence of that.

Weir believes that the marriage may have failed early on and that the fact that George possessed Lefèvre's translation of a satire on women and marriage, "Les Lamentations de Matheolous", perhaps speaks of his own views on women and marriage. Weir also wonders if Rochford subjected his wife to sexual practices like buggery and even though the rumours of George having a homosexual affair with Mark Smeaton are likely to be untrue, George may well have practised acts that were not seen as normal. Weir also writes that it may be significant that George and Jane's marriage was childless and that George Boleyn, Dean of Lichfield during the reign of Elizabeth I, was likely to have been an illegitimate son of George's, rather than a son of Jane. The fact that George had an affair with a woman seems to go against Retha Warnicke's view that George was homosexual. The Dean could, of course, have just been a Boleyn relative.

In George Cavendish's "Metrical Visions", Cavendish writes of George:-

> "I forced widows, maidens I did deflower.
> All was one to me, I spared none at all,
> My appetite was all women to devour
> My study was both day and hour."

which suggests that George was a womaniser, rather than someone known for buggery and illegal acts.

So, who was George?

Well, no real evidence points to him being a "libertine", and I would sum him up as:-

- A fervent religious reformer

- A poet and lover of the Arts

- An accomplished diplomat and politician

- A man who, like many other courtiers, took advantage of his position at court and enjoyed affairs with women at court

- A man who enjoyed his high position at court and who threw himself into his work

- A man who was close to his sister and enjoyed spending time with her and with others who shared their beliefs and passions

Notes and Sources

- Letters and Papers, Foreign and Domestic, Henry VIII
- Calendar of State Papers, Spain The Privy Purse Expenses of King Henry the Eighth, from November 1529, to December 1532 edited by Nicholas Harris
- "The Lady in the Tower" by Alison Weir
- "The Life and Death of Anne Boleyn" by Eric Ives
- "The Rise and Fall of Anne Boleyn" by Retha Warnicke
- "The Early Loves of Anne Boleyn" by Josephine Wilkinson
- "Jane Boleyn: The True Story of the Infamous Lady Rochford" by Julia Fox
- Metrical Visions, The Life of Cardinal Wolsey, George Cavendish

George Boleyn, Lord Rochford, Part 2

Louise, who commented on my first article on George Boleyn, made a very good point when she said that George Cavendish's words in "Metrical Visions" about George, and the other men, may well have been misinterpreted. As Louise says, Cavendish uses terms such as "bestial" and "unlawful lechery" frequently in his writing to sum up any behaviour that he considers inappropriate and he even referred to the King's "unlawful lechery". Would he dare to suggest that the King was a sodomite? No.

So why do historians assume that Cavendish is talking about buggery and bestiality when he writes about men like George? It may well be that George committed adultery, and was a bit of a womaniser, but there does not seem to be any evidence of him being homosexual or bisexual, whatever authors would have us believe.

I'm going to look at how a man who had risen to the point of holding one of the most influential posts in the Kingdom (the post of Warden of the Cinque Ports), could end up being accused of committing incest and treason, being executed for treason and having his body buried at the Tower's chapel, rather than in a nice family vault. A sad end to a very promising life.

A Warning Sign

The first sign that George Boleyn, Lord Rochford, was losing royal favour was on the 29th April 1536. It was expected that on this day George was going to be made a Knight of the Garter, but, to the horror of Anne, George and the Boleyn faction, Henry VIII had a change of heart and appointed Sir Nicholas Carew, a supporter of the King's mistress, Jane Seymour, as a Knight of the Garter. This was a shock for Anne and George and was a warning sign that things were swinging in Jane Seymour's favour and that Anne was losing her power over the King.

What Anne Boleyn, her brother and the Boleyn faction did

not know was that Cromwell had been cooking up a plot, not only to get rid of Anne, but to get rid of the entire Boleyn faction.

There are various theories about Cromwell's plot. Some, like Alison Weir, believe that the plot was Cromwell's doing and that the King was just as much of an innocent party as those who were plotted against. She believes that Cromwell was able to provide the King with enough evidence for him to believe that Anne was guilty, that she had betrayed him, and that is why Henry was able to support Cromwell's plans, see Anne and his favourites executed and move on to his new life with Jane Seymour. However, other historians believe that Henry VIII was actually complicit in Cromwell's plans, that he may well have ordered Cromwell's investigations and that he wanted rid of Anne.

Elizabeth Norton, author of "Anne Boleyn: Henry VIII's Obsession", said in our Anne Boleyn Files interview:-

"Henry VIII remained, until the end of his life, in full control of his kingdom. The plot against Catherine Parr, in which she was very nearly sent to the Tower for heresy in 1546 shows that it was not possible for Henry's wives to fall without his express agreement. Henry's seeming compliance in agreeing to Catherine's arrest was part of a test of his wife and an attempt to push her back into a more domestic sphere.

In contrast, Anne Boleyn was allowed to fall and there is evidence that Henry had tired of her. Whilst he did still seek Imperial recognition of his marriage to Anne as late as April 1536, it is clear that he was already by then becoming more committed to Jane Seymour – he perhaps simply had not found the mechanism by which to engineer Anne's fall. Cromwell and the other factions working against Anne provided the means by which she could be brought down, with the rumours of infidelity and the precontract with Henry Percy. It was Henry VIII himself who had to agree to the final attack on Anne and, his conduct at the May Day jousts shows that he did indeed agree to this."

It also would have been dangerous for Cromwell to move against the King's wife and royal favourites, such as George Boleyn and Sir Henry Norris, without the King's knowledge and blessing.

George Boleyn's Arrest

Mark Smeaton was invited to dine at Sir Thomas Cromwell's house in Stepney on the 30th April. This was far from being the lavish dinner that Smeaton anticipated and, instead of dinner, Smeaton was interrogated and may even have been tortured. As a result of this interrogation, Smeaton confessed to adultery with Anne Boleyn and it was this confession, however forced, that meant that Cromwell could move against Anne.

The next day, at the May Day jousts, the King is said to have received a message which caused him to leave abruptly, taking Sir Henry Norris along with him. Norris's man servant, George Constantine, wrote of how the King himself interrogated Norris on this journey back to Greenwich. Norris was taken to the Tower of London at dawn on the 2nd May and Eustace Chapuys wrote of how Smeaton was taken to the Tower on the morning on the 2nd and George Boleyn was taken after dinner (dinner was served between 10am and 1pm according to Alison Weir), "more than six hours after the others". Weir points out that George was arrested "so discreetly" that very few people knew about it. Weir also writes that it appears that George was arrested and taken to the Tower without being interrogated.

The Role of Lady Rochford

Much has been made, in fiction and on TV, of the role of Jane Boleyn (nee Parker), Lady Rochford, in the fall of George Boleyn and Anne Boleyn. If we are to believe the likes of Philippa Gregory and The Tudors, then we would see Jane as a bitter and vengeful woman who was jealous of George and Anne's close relationship and who wanted revenge for George's treatment of her.

Some historians believe that George and Jane's marriage was loveless and that Jane grew to hate George. Others believe that it was like any other marriage, with its ups and downs. Jane was one of

Anne's ladies and had actually conspired with Anne in 1534 to try and get Henry VIII's new mistress banished from court. However, it was Jane who was banished from court, for her part in the plot. Perhaps this turned Jane against Anne – who knows? It does appear though that Jane had a role in George and Anne's downfalls.

Eric Ives certainly blames her in part, writing of how she told the Crown about Anne's comments concerning Henry's impotence and that Lancelot de Carles recorded that Rochford said to the judges, "On the evidence of only one woman you are willing to believe this great evil of me, and on the basis of her allegations you are deciding my judgement." He points out the Portuguese report which told of "that person who more out of envy and jealousy than out of love towards the king did betray this accursed secret and together with it the names of those who had joined in the evil doings of the unchaste queen", as well as the lost journal of Antony Antony which described Jane as "a particular instrument in the death of Queen Anne."

Ives also writes that Bishop Burnet, who wasn't a contemporary of Anne and George but who had access to primary sources, asserted that Jane gave evidence of an inappropriate "familiarity" between Anne and George.

Alison Weir draws attention to George Wyatt's words regarding Jane, which can be found in his "The Life of Anne Boleigne":-

"For this principal matter between the queen and her brother, there was brought forth, indeed, witness, his wicked wife accuser of her own husband, even to the seeking of his blood, which I believe is hardly to be showed of any honest woman ever done. But of her, the judgment that fell out upon her, and the just punishment by law after of her naughtiness, show that' what she did was more to be rid of him than of true ground against him."

But, why would Jane do this to her husband and sister-in-law? Possible reasons could include:-

- Jealousy of George and Anne's close relationship
- Revenge on Anne for Jane's banishment from court

- Jane's family's connection to the Lady Mary – Weir writes of how Jane's father, Lord Morley, was sympathetic to the Lady Mary's cause.

- Jane's family's dislike of the Boleyns – Alison Weir writes of how Lord Morley had spent a few years in the household of Henry VIII's grandmother, Lady Margaret Beaufort, and would have known her great friend and confessor, John Fisher, Bishop of Rochester, who was executed on 22nd June 1535 for refusing to sign the oath of succession and refusing to recognise the King as the Supreme Head of the Church. Morley could well have blamed Anne Boleyn and her faction for Fisher's execution and Weir writes that the Parkers may have swapped sides from the Boleyns to Lady Mary after being disillusioned by Anne and her faction

- Jane discovered that her husband was having a homosexual affair with Mark Smeaton – This is highly unlikely and the only evidence that could be used to link the two men is the fact that George gave Smeaton a book of poems, "Les Lamentations de Matheolus" and "Le Livre de Leesce" by Jean Lefevre. Retha Warnicke believes that the fact that this book was an attack on marriage and was an expensive manuscript is a sign that the two men were more than just friends. It is rather sad that a gift between friends can be seen in this way. Scribblings from Thomas Wyatt can also be found on this book so is Warnicke saying that he was homosexual too?

- Jane was subjected to sexual practices that shocked and upset her – There is no evidence of this and we do not know what went on in their marriage.

- George was a womaniser – We have no evidence of this apart from George Cavendish's words about George deflowering maidens and his sexual appetite.

- Jane realised that the Boleyns were on their way down – Perhaps Jane realised that the Boleyns were about to fall and wanted to save herself. Perhaps she saw that the only way to distance herself from Anne and George, and to save her own neck, was to give the King and Cromwell what they wanted, evidence.

- Jane was forced to give evidence – Perhaps we are misjudging Jane, perhaps she had no choice in the matter. It could well be that Cromwell put pressure on her and there was no way out for her. She could either go down with the Boleyns or do what Cromwell wanted.

But did Jane Boleyn even give evidence to Cromwell regarding George and Anne? Perhaps not.

Historian Dr John Guy, in his review of Alison Weir's "The Lady in the Tower" points out the flaws in the argument that Jane did give evidence and confessed to it at her own execution:-

- De Carles reported that "a single woman" produced the most damaging material against Anne and George, but de Carles hinted at Lady Worcester, not Jane. Although Weir and others think that he was confused, as Jane was interrogated at the time, Guy points out that there is no proof that it was Jane.

- Chapuys and a Portuguese gentleman – Guy writes that although Weir says that Chapuys named Jane as divulging the "accursed secret" in a letter, he does not actually say this and the Portuguese gentleman just talks of "that person" and does not name Jane.

- Jane's confession at her execution in 1542 is actually a forgery. Guy points out that an eye-witness account of Jane's execution makes no mention of this confession and the source that does mention it is known to be unreliable.

Weir is not the only historian to believe that Jane had a role in George and Anne's falls, Ives also gives sources to back this idea up. But perhaps we are being unfair on Jane, perhaps she was not the vengeful wife that many paint her to be. Perhaps she too was a victim, losing her husband and sister-in-law in such a tragic way. I guess we'll never know for sure, but I'm willing to give her the benefit of the doubt.

Notes and Sources

- Letters and Papers, Foreign and Domestic, Henry VIII – Found online at British History Online
- "Anne Boleyn: Henry VIII's Obsession" by Elizabeth Norton
- "The Lady in the Tower" by Alison Weir
- "The Life and Death of Anne Boleyn" by Eric Ives
- "The Rise and Fall of Anne Boleyn" by Retha Warnicke
- "The Early Loves of Anne Boleyn" by Josephine Wilkinson
- "Jane Boleyn: The True Story of the Infamous Lady Rochford" by Julia Fox
- "The Chronicle of Calais in the Reigns of Henry VII and Henry VIII to the year 1540" Edited by John Gough Nichols
- "The Lady in the Tower: The Fall of Anne Boleyn by Alison Weir – a Sunday Times Review by John Guy", 1st November 2009
- "The Life of Anne Boleigne" by George Wyatt in "The Life of Cardinal Wolsey" by George Cavendish
- "Excerpta Historica" by S Bentley, p261-262, Translation of a letter from a Portuguese gentleman to a friend in Lisbon describing the execution of Anne Boleyn, Lord Rocheford, Brereton, Norris, Smeton, and Weston

George Boleyn, Lord Rochford, Part 3

George Boleyn was arrested on the 2nd May, the day after the May Day jousts, and taken to the Tower of London to await trial.

The part of the Middlesex Indictment relating to George Boleyn says:-

"Also that the Queen, 2 Nov.27 Hen.VIII [1535] and several times before and after, by the means therein stated, procured and incited her own natural brother, George Boleyn, knight, Lord Rochford, to violate her, alluring him with her tongue in the said George's mouth, and the said George's tongue in hers, and also with kisses, presents and jewels, against the commands of God, and all laws human and divine, whereby her, despising the commands of God, and all other human laws, 5 Nov.27 Henry VIII [1535], violated and carnally knew the said Queen, his own sister, at Westminster, which he also did on divers days before and after, sometimes by his own procurement and sometimes by the Queen's...Moreover, the said Lord Rochford, Norris, Brereton, Weston and Smeaton, being thus inflamed with carnal love of the Queen, and having become very jealous of each other, gave her secret gifts and pledges while carrying on this illicit intercourse..."

The indictment of the Grand Jury of Kent accused Anne of soliciting George on 22nd December 1535 at Eltham Palace, committing incest with him there on the 29th December and compassing the King's death with him, Norris, Weston and Brereton on 8th January 1536 at Greenwich.

Alison Weir writes of how accusing Anne and George of incest in November 1535 may have been intended to imply that George was the father of the child that Anne miscarried in 1536.

Both Eric Ives and Alison Weir state that many of the charges against Anne were impossible, due to her being in different places or with the King on the dates mentioned, but however illogical these dates and charges were, Anne, George and the four other men were all found guilty and sentenced to death.

George Boleyn's Trial

Norris, Brereton, Smeaton and Weston were tried as commoners at a special sessions of oyer and terminer on the 12th May at Westminster Hall and then the Queen, Anne Boleyn, was tried on Monday 15th May in the King's Hall at the Tower of London, by a jury of her peers, with George following directly after. The fact that Norris, Smeaton, Brereton and Weston were all found guilty of adultery with the Queen meant that the trials of George and Anne were extremely prejudiced – how could they be found innocent now?

On 15th May, the Letters and Paper, Foreign and Domestic, Henry VIII (LP 10.876) tell us that the Duke of Norfolk, the uncle of Anne and George, was the Lord High Steward presiding over the trial and that the panel consisted of:-

"Charles duke of Suffolk, Hen. marquis of Exeter, Will. earl of Arundel, John earl of Oxford, Hen. earl of Northumberland, Ralph earl of Westmoreland, Edw. earl of Derby, Hen. earl of Worcester, Thos. earl of Rutland, Rob. earl of Sussex, Geo. earl of Huntingdon, John lord Audeley, Thos. lord La Ware, Hen. lord Mountague, Hen. lord Morley, Thos. lord Dacre, Geo. lord Cobham, Hen. lord Maltravers, Edw. lord Powes, Thos. lord Mount Egle, Edw. lord Clynton, Will. lord Sandes, Andrew lord Wyndesore, Thos. lord Wentworth, Thos. lord Burgh, and John lord Mordaunt."

The Letters and Papers (LP 10.876) go on to say of Anne:-

"And afterwards, Monday, 15 May, queen Anne comes to the bar before the Lord High Steward in the Tower, in the custody of Sir Will. Kingston, pleads not guilty, and puts herself on her peers; whereupon the said duke of Suffolk, marquis of Exeter, and other peers, are charged by the High Steward to say the truth; and being examined from the lowest peer to the highest, each of them severally saith that she is guilty.

Judgment:—To be taken to prison in the Tower, and then, at the King's command, to the Green within the Tower, and there to be burned or beheaded as shall please the King."

Straight after Anne's trial was George's trial and the Letters and Papers say of George's trial:-

"The same day, lord Rocheford is brought before the High Steward in the custody of Sir Will. Kingston, and pleads not guilty. The peers are charged, with the exception of the earl of Northumberland, who was suddenly taken ill, and each of them severally saith that he is guilty.

Judgment:—To be taken to prison in the Tower, and then drawn through the city of London, to the gallows at Tyburn, &c., as usual in high treason."

Charles Wriothesley recorded that after George pleaded not guilty, "he made answer so prudently and wisely to all articles laid against him, that marvel it was to hear, but never would confess anything, but made himself as clear as though he had never offended" and Lancelot de Carles wrote of "his calm behaviour and good defence. More [Thomas More] himself did not reply better".

Elizabeth Norton, in her book "Anne Boleyn: Henry VIII's Obsession", quotes Chapuys as saying the evidence presented for the charge of incest was that George had once spent a long time visiting his sister – was a man not meant to spend time with his sister?! Norton writes of how George was contemptuous in dismissing the evidence and no wonder! George was also charged, like Anne had been, with having laughed at the King and the clothes he wore, something that Norton feels that Anne and George could have been guilty of because of their own stylish way of dressing.

In a letter from Chapuys to Charles V, written on 19th May (LP 10.908), Chapuys writes:-

"I must not omit, that among other things charged against him as a crime was, that his sister had told his wife that the King "nestoit habile en cas de soy copuler avec femme, et quil navoit ne vertu ne puissance." This he was not openly charged with, but it was shown him in writing, with a warning not to repeat it. But he immediately declared the matter, in great contempt of Cromwell and some others, saying he would not in this point arouse any suspicion which might prejudice the King's issue. He was also charged with having spread reports which called in question whether his sister's daughter was the King's child."

The French in this quote translates to mean that Henry VIII was not able to have sexual intercourse with a woman because he lacked the potency and vigour, i.e. he was impotent. As Chapuys writes, George was instructed not to read this out in court but by this George did not care and he rebelliously and contemptuously read it out. Norton points out that the Act of Succession made this kind of talk, and his gossip over whether Elizabeth was the King's daughter, treason because it impugned the King's issue.

George defended himself as strongly and eloquently as Anne had done and Chapuys wrote:-

"Her brother was charged with having cohabited with her by presumption, because he had been once found a long time with her, and with certain other little follies. To all he replied so well that several of those present wagered 10 to 1 that he would be acquitted, especially as no witnesses were produced against either him or her, as it is usual to do, particularly when the accused denies the charge." (LP 10.908)

No witnesses and an eloquent defence, but George was still found guilty:-

"Her brother, after his condemnation, said that since he must die, he would no longer maintain his innocence, but confessed that he had deserved death. He only begged the King that his debts, which he recounted, might be paid out of his goods." (Chapuys LP 10.908)

What do Chapuys' words mean though? Do they mean that once he was condemned, George confessed to incest? No, I don't think so. I think George was just admitting that he, as a sinner, deserved judgement from God. I don't think we should read too much into Chapuys' words. As Leanda de Lisle explains, in her book "The Sisters Who Would be Queen", people convicted of a crime believe that they deserved death and that it was a punishment from God for their sinful life, even if they were innocent of the crime they were convicted of.

George Boleyn's Execution

On the morning of Wednesday 17th May, George Boleyn, Norris, Weston, Brereton and Smeaton were led out of the Tower to a scaffold on Tower Hill. George Boleyn, Lord Rochford, was the highest in rank and so was the first to be executed. Letters and Papers (LP 10.911) has the following record:-

"The count (viscount) Rochefort, brother of the queen (unjustly so called) Anne Boleyn, was beheaded with an axe upon a scaffold before the Tower of London. He made a very catholic address to the people, saying he had not come thither to preach, but to serve as a mirror and example, acknowledging his sins against God and the King, and declaring he need not recite the causes why he was condemned, as it could give no pleasure to hear them. He first desired mercy and pardon of God, and afterwards of the King and all others whom he might have offended, and hoped that men would not follow the vanities of the world and the flatteries of the Court, which had brought him to that shameful end. He said if he had followed the teachings of the Gospel, which he had often read, he would not have fallen into this danger, for a good doer was far better than a good reader. In the end, he pardoned those who had condemned him to death, and asked the people to pray for his soul."

The Spanish Chronicle says:-

"Then the Duke turned to the people and said in the hearing of many "I beg you to pray to God for me; for by the trial I have to pass through I am blameless, and never even knew that my sister was bad. Guiltless as I am, I pray God to have mercy upon my soul. " Then he lay upon the ground with his head on the block, the headsman gave three strokes, and so died this poor duke." (" Chronicle of King Henry VIII of England", translated by Martin A Sharp Hume P67)

The Chronicle of Calais records George Boleyn's execution speech as:-

"Christen men, I am borne undar the lawe, and judged undar

the lawe, and dye undar the lawe, and the lawe hathe condemned me. Mastars all, I am not come hether for to preche, but for to dye, for I have deserved for to dye yf I had xx. lyves, more shamefully than can be devysed, for I am a wreched synnar, and I have synned shamefully, I have knowne no man so evell, and to reherse my synnes openly it were no pleaswre to you to here them, nor yet for me to reherse them, for God knowethe all; therefore, mastars all, I pray yow take hede by me, and especially my lords and gentlemen of the cowrte, the whiche I have bene amonge, take hede by me, and beware of suche a fall, and I pray to God the Fathar, the Sonne, and the Holy Ghoste, thre persons and one God, that my deathe may be an example unto yow all, and beware, trust not in the vanitie of the worlde, and especially in the flateringe of the cowrte. And I cry God mercy, and aske all the worlde forgevenes, as willingly as I wowld have forgevenes of God ; and yf I have offendyd any man that is not here now, eythar in thowght, worde, or dede, and yf ye here any suche, I pray yow hertely in my behalfe, pray them to forgyve me for God's sake. And yet, my mastars all, I have one thinge for to say to yow, men do comon and saye that I have bene a settar forthe of the worde of God, and one that have favored the Ghospell of Christ ; and bycawse I would not that God's word shuld be slaundered by me, I say unto yow all, that yf I had followed God's worde in dede as I dyd rede it and set it forthe to my power, I had not come to this. I dyd red the Ghospell of Christe, but I dyd not follow it; yf I had, I had bene a lyves man amonge yow : therefore I pray yow, mastars all, for God's sake sticke to the trwthe and folowe it, for one good followere is worthe thre redars, as God knowethe."

(The Chronicle of Calais In the Reigns of Henry VII and Henry VIII to the Year 1540, edited by John Gough Nichols, page 46)

The editor of The Chronicle of Calais points out that this speech is very similar to the one given in the Excerpta Historica, 1831, in a contemporary account by a Portuguese man.

I get goosebumps when I think of the three blows that it is said to have taken for the headsman to finish George off. An execution by beheading is a scary enough death but prisoners always hoped that they would die from one swift, clean blow. Three sounds rather awful.

Once the men had been executed and their bodies stripped of their clothing, George, as a nobleman, was taken to the Chapel of St Peter ad Vincula where, according to John Whitcombe Bayley in "The History and Antiquities of the Tower of London", Rochford's head and body were interred before the high altar.

George Boleyn's Legacy

George and Anne were dead and gone, but they left behind a family who were lucky to escape Cromwell's coup against Anne and the Boleyn faction.

- Thomas Boleyn, Earl of Wiltshire – George and Anne's father had escaped with his head and neck intact and remained on the King's Council, but he lost his position as Lord Privy Seal in June 1536. Alison Weir writes of how there is record of him attending the christening of Prince Edward in October 1537, lending Cromwell his garter insignia and helping to suppress the Pilgrimage of Grace in 1537. Although there were rumours of him marrying Lady Margaret Douglas, the King's niece, after his wife's death, he never remarried and actually died on 12th March 1539 at Hever, one year after his wife.

- Elizabeth Boleyn (née Howard) – Elizabeth died in April 1538 and was given a lavish funeral.

- Mary Boleyn – Mary, the sister of George and Anne, died on 30th July 1543 in relative obscurity, possibly at Rochford Hall in Essex. She left behind her husband, William Stafford, and her children Henry and Catherine Carey.

- George Boleyn, Dean of Lichfield – This man was Dean of Lichfield under Elizabeth I and described himself in his will as a relative of Elizabeth's cousin Henry Carey, Lord Hunsdon. Although some believe that he was George's son, he never claimed to be so and also Thomas Boleyn's estate passed to Mary Boleyn, not to him.

- Jane Boleyn, Lady Rochford – After George Boleyn's execution, his goods and assets were seized by the crown and Jane was left in financial difficulties, so difficult that she wrote a letter in that same year begging Cromwell for help. At the end of May 1536, there is record of this letter in Letters and Papers (10.1010), saying "Jane, widow of Lord Rochford, to [Cromwell]. Beseeching him to obtain from the King for her the stuff and plate of her husband. The King and her father paid 2,000 marks for her jointure to the earl of Wyltchere, and she is only assured of 100 marks during the Earl's life, "which is very hard for me to shift the world withal." Prays him to inform the King of this. Signed."

  There is evidence that Cromwell did help Jane and by the end of 1536 she was back at court working as a lady-in-waiting to the new Queen, Jane Seymour. Jane Rochford carried on at court, serving Jane, then Anne of Cleves and Catherine Howard until she was executed on 13th February 1542, along with Catherine Howard, for acting as a go-between for the Queen and her lover, Thomas Culpepper. Those who believe that she falsely accused Anne and George of incest may feel that she got her come-uppance.

- Elizabeth I, daughter of Anne Boleyn and niece of George Boleyn – The little girl who was just two years and 8 months old when he mother and uncle were executed on her father's orders was to become one of the greatest monarchs in English history. What a legacy!

Whatever we think of George Boleyn, his personal life and behaviour – whether you believe that he was a reckless libertine or that he was a talented diplomat and poet – George Boleyn did not deserve to die a gruesome death on the block and to still have his reputation maligned today. In my eyes, he was a highly intelligent man who was passionate about religious reform and the Arts. He was a man of his time in that he probably had an unhappy arranged marriage and may well have enjoyed the odd dalliance on the side, but his rise at court and his popularity shows that he was held in high esteem by those around him and the King trusted him with highly sensitive information and important jobs.

I leave you with the words of another poet, Thomas Wyatt, who wrote about the executions of the five men in his poem "In Mourning Wise Since Daily I Increase":-

> As for them all I do not thus lament,
> But as of right my reason doth me bind;
> But as the most doth all their deaths repent,
> Even so do I by force of mourning mind.
> Some say, 'Rochford, haddest thou been not so proud,
> For thy great wit each man would thee bemoan,
> Since as it is so, many cry aloud
> It is great loss that thou art dead and gone.'

Notes and Sources

- Letters and Papers, Foreign and Domestic, Henry VIII – Found online at British History Online
- "Anne Boleyn: Henry VIII's Obsession" by Elizabeth Norton
- "The Lady in the Tower" by Alison Weir
- "The Life and Death of Anne Boleyn" by Eric Ives
- "The Rise and Fall of Anne Boleyn" by Retha Warnicke
- "The Early Loves of Anne Boleyn" by Josephine Wilkinson
- "Jane Boleyn: The True Story of the Infamous Lady Rochford" by Julia Fox
- "The Chronicle of Calais in the Reigns of Henry VII and Henry VIII to the year 1540" Edited by John Gough Nichols
- "Chronicle of King Henry VIII of England" translated by

Martin A Sharp Hume

- Charles Wriothesley's "A Chronicle of England During the Reigns of the Tudors from AD 1485-1559"

- "Excerpta Historica" by S Bentley, p261-262, Translation of a letter from a Portuguese gentleman to a friend in Lisbon describing the execution of Anne Boleyn, Lord Rocheford, Brereton, Norris, Smeton, and Weston

- "The History and Antiquities of the Tower of London", John Whitcombe Bayley, 1821

17th May 1536 -The Deaths of 5 Men and a Marriage Destroyed

On the 17th May 1536, Sir Henry Norris, Sir Francis Weston, Mark Smeaton, Sir William Brereton and George Boleyn, Lord Rochford were led out of the Tower of London to a scaffold which had been erected on Tower Hill. I cannot imagine how they felt as they surveyed the scene and realised that death was closing in on them. Their only comfort was that they were all to be beheaded, a much more merciful death than being hanged, drawn and quartered.

I will now examine each man's execution in the order that they were said to have been killed.

George Boleyn, Lord Rochford

As the highest in rank, Anne Boleyn's brother, George Boleyn, Lord Rochford, was the first to be executed and at least he did not have to watch as his friends and colleagues were killed one by one. Before he knelt at the block, he made a speech, but it is hard to know exactly what he said when there are a few different versions of his final speech.

According to a Spanish record in Letters and Papers:-

"The count (viscount) Rochefort, brother of the queen (unjustly so called) Anne Boleyn, was beheaded with an axe upon a scaffold before the Tower of London. He made a very catholic address to the people, saying he had not come thither to preach, but to serve as a mirror and example, acknowledging his sins against God and the King, and declaring he need not recite the causes why he was condemned, as it could give no pleasure to hear them. He first desired mercy and pardon of God, and afterwards of the King and all others whom he might have offended, and hoped that men would not follow the vanities of the world and the flatteries of the Court, which had brought him to that shameful end. He said if he had followed the teachings of the Gospel, which he had often read, he would not have fallen into this danger, for a good doer was far better than a good reader. In the end, he pardoned those who had condemned him to death, and asked the people to pray for his soul."[1]

The Chronicle of King Henry VIII (The Spanish Chronicle) says:-

"Then the Duke turned to the people and said in the hearing of many "I beg you to pray to God for me; for by the trial I have to pass through I am blameless, and never even knew that my sister was bad. Guiltless as I am, I pray God to have mercy upon my soul." Then he lay upon the ground with his head on the block, the headsman gave three strokes, and so died this poor duke."[2]

The Chronicle of Calais records George Boleyn's execution speech as:-

"Christen men, I am borne undar the lawe, and judged undar the lawe, and dye undar the lawe, and the lawe hathe condemned me. Mastars all, I am not come hether for to preche, but for to dye, for I have deserved for to dye yf I had xx. lyves, more shamefully than can be devysed, for I am a wreched synnar, and I have synned shamefully, I have knowne no man so evell, and to reherse my synnes openly it were no pleaswre to you to here them, nor yet for me to reherse them, for God knowethe all; therefore, mastars all, I pray yow take hede by me, and especially my lords and gentlemen of the cowrte, the whiche I have bene amonge, take hede by me, and beware of suche a fall, and I pray to God the Fathar, the Sonne, and the Holy Ghoste, thre persons and one God, that my deathe may be an example unto yow all, and beware, trust not in the vanitie of the worlde, and especially in the flateringe of the cowrte. And I cry God mercy, and aske all the worlde forgevenes, as willingly as I wowld have forgevenes of God; and yf I have offendyd any man that is not here now, eythar in thowght, worde, or dede, and yf ye here any suche, I pray yow hertely in my behalfe, pray them to forgyve me for God's sake. And yet, my mastars all, I have one thinge for to say to yow, men do comon and saye that I have bene a settar forthe of the worde of God, and one that have favored the Ghospell of Christ ; and bycawse I would not that God's word shuld be slaundered by me, I say unto yow all, that yf I had followecl God's worde in dede as I dyd rede it and set it forthe to my power, I had not come to this. I dyd red the Ghospell of Christe, but I dyd not follow it; yf I had, I had bene a lyves man amonge yow : therefore I pray yow, mastars all, for God's sake sticke to the trwthe and folowe it, for one good followere is worthe thre redars, as God knowethe."[3]

The editor of The Chronicle of Calais points out that this speech is very similar to the one given in the Excerpta Historica, 1831, in a contemporary account by a Portuguese man. My favourite speech is this one. George followed convention by acknowledging that he had been condemned by the law and confessing that he was a sinner who deserved death, but then, although he started by saying that he was not going to preach a sermon, he then spoke what Eric Ives describes as "the language of Zion"[4], urging those witnessing his death to "stick to the truth and follow it", and not make the mistakes that he had. Powerful words indeed and spoken by a man who believed that he was justified by faith even though he may not have had the most perfect of lives.

George then knelt at the block and was beheaded. I do hope that the Spanish Chronicle is wrong when it says that three strokes were required.

Sir Henry Norris

As the next in rank, Sir Henry Norris followed George Boleyn on to the scaffold. George Constantine, Norris's manservant and a witness of these bloody events, recorded that "the others confessed, all but Mr Norris, who said almost nothing at all.[5] I do not think that he means that they confessed that they had slept with Anne Boleyn, more that they had confessed that they were sinners, as was the done thing at executions. However, Gilbert Burnet, Bishop of Salisbury, wrote of Norris saying:-

"I do not think that any gentleman of the court owes more to [the King] than I do, and hath been more ungrateful and regardless of it than I have"[6]

and then defending the Queen:

"loyally averred that in his conscience, he thought the Queen innocent of these things laid to her charge; but whether she was or not, he would not accuse her of any thing, and he would die a thousand times rather than ruin an innocent person."[7]

The Spanish Chronicle reported that Sir Henry Norris "made a great long prayer" and declared that he deserved death because he had been ungrateful to the King. He then knelt at the block and was executed

Sir Francis Weston

Sir Francis Weston was the third of the men to be executed and before he knelt at the bloody block he said

"I had thought to live in abomination yet this twenty or thirty years, and then to have made amends, I thought little I would come to this."

He then added that the people gathered should learn "by example of him"[8].

Weston's speech is different in that he mentions living in "abomination", rather than being just a plain common and garden sinner. As I have said before, in previous articles on Weston, I think it is reading too much into his words to see him as someone who was homosexual, as Retha Warnicke would have us believe, or even, as Weir says, someone who had committed "illicit sexual acts". [9] In my opinion, Weston is just referring to the fact that he, like everyone, was a sinner and that he had hoped to have had an opportunity to have put things right and to live a better life. We probably all wish that when faced with death.

He then knelt at the bloodsoaked block and his life was taken.

Sir William Brereton

Sir William Brereton was the fourth man to climb the scaffold. According to The Spanish Chronicle, he simply said "I have offended God and the King; pray for me", but George Constantine recorded him saying:-

"I have deserved to dye if it were a thousande deethes. But the cause wherfore I dye judge not: But yf ye judge, judge the best."[10]

Was Brereton simply exaggerating in his fear or do his words about deserving a thousand deaths suggest that he had led a criminal life and perhaps been involved in sodomy and illicit sexual acts? I cannot see any evidence for Retha Warnicke's view that all five men were libertines who committed sodomy on a regular basis, but it does appear that Brereton was a bit of a Tudor bad boy, someone who I described in one article as being "a womaniser who protected murderers and used his influence for revenge". Perhaps his rather colourful past and less than perfect lifestyle caused him to suffer a pang of guilt on the scaffold.

Norris's servant George Constantine wrote of how Brereton repeated "But if ye judge, judge the best" three or four times and Constantine felt that "if he were gyltie, I say therfore that he dyed worst of them all",[11] meaning that if Brereton had been guilty then he would surely have confessed his guilt and asked God's forgiveness, rather than risking eternal damnation by dying with unconfessed sin.

Mark Smeaton

Mark Smeaton was the final man to be executed and how awful to have seen those three men die such violent deaths in front of him, knowing that he only had minutes to live. In "The Lady in the Tower", Alison Weir describes how the scaffold and block must have been completely soaked in blood by the time Smeaton climbed up there and, of course, his friends' bodies would also be in full view. According to George Constantine[12], Smeaton said:-

"Masters, I pray you all pray for me, for I have deserved the death."

And then he was beheaded. He did not take the opportunity to retract his confession and when Anne heard of this she said:-

"Did he not exonerate me," she said, "before he died, of the public infamy he laid on me? Alas! I fear his soul will suffer for it."[13]

The bodies were stripped and prepared for burial. Norris, Smeaton, Brereton and Weston, as commoners, were buried in the churchyard of the Chapel of St Peter ad Vincula, but George Boleyn's head and body were taken inside the Chapel, where, according to John Whitcombe Bayley,[14] they were interred before the high altar. Just two days later his sister's head and body would be joining him.

A Marriage Destroyed

Also on the 17th May 1536 at Lambeth, Archbishop Thomas Cranmer, in the presence of Sir Thomas Audley, the Duke of Suffolk, the Earl of Oxford and other, declared that the marriage between Henry VIII and Anne Boleyn was null and void.[15] It was as if they had never been married and Henry VIII was now free to marry again and there was a woman waiting in the wings.

Notes and Sources

1. L&P x.911

2. "The Chronicle of King Henry VIII of England", translated by Martin A Sharp Hume P67

3. The Chronicle of Calais In the Reigns of Henry VII and Henry VIII to the Year 1540, edited by John Gough Nichols, page 46

4. The Life and Death of Anne Boleyn, Eric Ives, p278

5. A Memorial from George Constantyne to Thomas Lord Cromwell

6. History of the Reformation, Gilbert Burnet

7. Ibid

8. Ibid.

9. The Lady in the Tower, Alison Weir

10. A Memorial from George Constantyne to Thomas Lord Cromwell

11. Ibid.

12. Ibid.

13. LP x. 1036

14. The History and Antiquities of the Tower of London, John Whitcomb Bayley, p120

15. L&P x.896

19th May 1536 – I Have a Little Neck.
The Execution of Anne Boleyn

At dawn on the 19th May 1536, Anne celebrated the Mass for the last time, receiving the Sacrament from her almoner, John Skip. She then ate breakfast at 7am and waited to hear Sir William Kingston's footsteps outside her door. At 8am, the Constable appeared, informing Anne that the hour of her death was near and that she should get herself ready, but Anne was already prepared.

Dressed in a robe of grey or black damask trimmed with ermine, with a crimson kirtle underneath and an English style gable hood, Anne took her final walk out of the Queen's Lodgings. She walked past the Great Hall, through Cole Harbour Gate, along the western side of the White Tower to the black draped scaffold. Kingston helped her up the scaffold steps and Anne stepped forward to address the crowd which included many people she knew – Thomas Cromwell, Charles Brandon, Duke of Suffolk, Henry Fitzroy, Duke of Richmond (Henry VIII's son), and Thomas Audley, the Lord Chancellor. The crowd fell silent as they gazed at their queen, who one witness described as being "never so beautiful". Anne then gave her final speech:-

"Good Christian people, I have not come here to preach a sermon; I have come here to die. For according to the law and by the law I am judged to die, and therefore I will speak nothing against it. I am come hither to accuse no man, nor to speak of that whereof I am accused and condemned to die, but I pray God save the King and send him long to reign over you, for a gentler nor a more merciful prince was there never, and to me he was ever a good, a gentle, and sovereign lord. And if any person will meddle of my cause, I require them to judge the best. And thus I take my leave of the world and of you all, and I heartily desire you all to pray for me."

She did not protest her innocence and preach to the crowd

as her brother had, she simply did what was expected of her. Executions were carefully choreographed and there was a set format for execution speeches and Anne followed it to the letter. There was no way that she would risk her daughter's safety by defying the King and proclaiming her innocence, Elizabeth's safety and her future relationship with her father, the King, were paramount in Anne's mind as she prepared to meet her Maker.

Her ladies then removed Anne's mantle and Anne lifted off her gable hood and tucked her famous dark locks into a cap to keep it out of the way of the sword. Eric Ives writes of how her only show of fear was the way that she kept looking behind her to check that the executioner was not going to strike the fatal blow too soon. Anne paid the executioner, he asked Anne's forgiveness and then Anne knelt upright in the straw, praying all the while "O Lord have mercy on me, to God I commend my soul. To Jesus Christ I commend my soul; Lord Jesu receive my soul." As Anne prayed, the executioner called out to his assistant to pass him his sword and, as Anne moved her head to follow what the assistant was doing, the executioner came up unnoticed behind her and beheaded her with one stroke of his sword. Her ordeal was over – her head may have been in the straw but Anne's soul was with her Father in Heaven.

As the shocked crowd dispersed, Anne's ladies wrapped her head and body in white cloth and took them to the Chapel of St Peter ad Vincula, where she was placed inside a old elm chest which had once contained bow staves. Anne Boleyn, Queen of England and mother of Elizabeth I, was then buried as a traitor in an unmarked grave.

Notes and Sources

- The Life of Anne Boleigne, George Wyatt, in The Life of Cardinal Wolsey, 214
- Hall's Chronicle, p819

Anne Boleyn – All Things to All People

This article was sparked off by a comment on Facebook from a lady who was a stripper and admired Anne Boleyn because "she played Henry like a lute.... she got the cash, the jewels, and the crown... Anne didn't take his shit. She was his equal." I immediately found myself getting on my soapbox and high horse, writing of how the primary sources did not support this idea of Anne blah blah blah, but then I stopped and deleted my comment. I thought "Who am I to tell this woman, who obviously admires Anne and says that she has been her role model since she was a little girl, what to believe about Anne?" Although that's not 'my' Anne Boleyn, can I prove definitively that Anne wasn't the woman that lady believes in? Hmmm...

It got me thinking that the beauty of Anne Boleyn, the thing that draws us in and won't let go, is her mystery and the fact that she can be all things to all people.

For some, she is a feminist icon, for others she is a tragic victim. For some she is a Protestant martyr, for others she is the victim of a faction battle. For some she is a sexual predator, for others she is a manipulated pawn on a chessboard or a victim of sexual harassment. For some she is a whore and a home-wrecker, for others she is a virtuous woman who dared to say "no". For some she is the proud, ambitious woman who played a game and deserved everything she got, for others she was a woman who made the best out of her situation. For some she is a role model who inspires them, for others she is the woman who stole another woman's husband and deserves to be damned for eternity. In Howard Brenton's play, she is the woman who caused the English Reformation, a Joan of Arc figure, and in The Other Boleyn Girl she is a scheming woman who will consider murder and incest to get what she wants....

Anne Boleyn is a paradox. Her life can be manipulated by historians and authors to fit their theories and ideas. The primary sources can be read in different ways. We fill in the blanks in her story with our own ideas about her, yet we just don't know who Anne Boleyn really was. We do not have a portrait that we can hand-on-heart say "that is Anne Boleyn", we do not have her replies to Henry VIII's love letters, we don't have a diary that she kept; all we have is contemporary sources, some written by people who admired her, e.g. John Foxe, and some written by those who did not care for her, e.g. Eustace Chapuys.

Then we have books written by learned academics, the likes of Eric Ives and G W Bernard, but even they don't agree. We have Ives, who believes that Anne Boleyn was innocent and that she was framed, arguing that the dates used in the indictments at her trial make no sense as she was not even at those places at those times, and then we have G W Bernard playing Devil's advocate and asking does that really prove that she was innocent? It seems that we can use the evidence to support completely opposite theories!

I have dedicated my time to finding out the 'real' truth about Anne Boleyn, but what is that? Will I ever find it? Can I paint the picture of the real Anne Boleyn? "No" is the honest answer. What I can do is research her life, look at the sources and interpret them but what I write is MY interpretation. OK, there are various acknowledged facts, things that appear in many different sources, but most of what we believe about Anne is based on hypotheses, whether our own or that of an historian. When we had history essays to write based on a statement which then ended with "Discuss", my history teacher at school (thank you, Mrs Sagi!) said that it did not matter what case you argued as long as you could back it up with evidence, and the mystery surrounding Anne Boleyn means that we can represent her in so many different ways and nobody can tell us that we are wrong.

Where does that leave those of us who are trying to get to the truth? It leaves us having to accept that Anne Boleyn is a puzzle, and loving her for that, it leaves us acknowledging that we are on a journey that may have no end.

Further Reading

Thank you for reading this book. You can, of course, read more at The Anne Boleyn Files but here are some books that I would also highly recommend:

- The Life and Death of Anne Boleyn, Eric Ives
- The Lady in the Tower, Alison Weir
- Six Wives: The Queens of Henry VIII, David Starkey
- Anne Boleyn In her Words and the Words of Those Who Knew Her, edited by Elizabeth Norton

Claire Ridgway

www.TheAnneBoleynFiles.com

Index

A

Adultery 11, 12, 34, 40, 80, 123, 138, 148, 154, 211, 213, 220
Anne Gainsford 169
Anne of Cleves 19, 59, 62, 75, 76, 77, 87, 171, 177
  Smell 61
Ashmolean Museum 190, 191, 192, 193, 197

B

Baynton, Sir Edward 183
Beaufort, Margaret 215
Betts, William 186
Bigamy 34, 40, 158
Blount, Bessie, Elizabeth 25, 132, 136
Boleyn, Anne 3, 7, 33, 101, 109, 114, 141, 153, 166, 229, 239
  Burial 95, 116, 121, 229
  Execution 96, 237
  Homewrecker 37
  Marriage 138
  Martyr 41
  Sexualization / Incest 105, 147
  Stereotype 3, 19
  Vampire 35
Boleyn, Elizabeth 9, 199, 225
Boleyn, George 9, 97, 147, 211, 219, 229
  Execution 223, 229
  Life at Court 202
  Poetry and Religion 206
  Trial 220
Boleyn, Henry 189, 197, 199, 201
Boleyn, James 182
Boleyn, Jane 10, 14, 73, 107, 121, 123, 213
  Appearance 48
Boleyn, Mary 7, 14, 101, 225
Boleyn, Thomas 189, 197, 199, 201, 225
Borough, Sir Thomas 84
Boudicca 107

Bourbon, Nicholas 14
Brandon, Catherine 89
Brandon, Charles 14, 41, 67, 71, 237
Brasted 202
Brenton, Howard 106, 239
Brereton, Sir William 97, 147, 152, 219, 220, 223, 229, 233
Browne, Elizabeth 175

C

Carew, Sir Nicholas 51, 56, 211
Carey, Catherine 225
Carey, Henry 13, 41, 225
Carey, William 8, 13, 41
Carles, Lancelot de 148, 150, 216, 221
Catherine of Aragon 12, 19, 21, 34, 48, 53, 87, 109, 129, 131, 135, 141, 154, 159, 164, 166, 176, 183, 202
  Appearance 22
Cavendish, George 135, 208, 211, 215
Chapuys, Eustace 4, 11, 28, 35, 49, 52, 63, 102, 103, 105, 109, 110, 153, 161, 162, 163, 164, 165, 166, 170, 182, 203, 213, 216
Charles V 35, 52, 144, 162, 203, 221
Cobham, Nan 171
Coffin, William 181
Constantine, George 213, 231, 233
Cranmer, Thomas 40, 77, 89, 157, 158, 160, 234
Cromwell, Thomas 14, 59, 74, 103, 149, 150, 154, 163, 182, 187, 205, 212, 216, 221, 225, 226
Cryche, Henry 184
Culpeper, Thomas 67, 68, 73, 75, 78, 80, 107, 151, 171

D

Dereham, Sir Francis 67, 69, 71, 72, 75, 77, 79, 80, 81, 97
Douglas, Margaret 176
Dymoke, Margaret 173

E

Edward VI 52, 53
Eleanor of Aquitaine 107
Elizabeth Holland 170
Elizabeth I, Lady 87, 107, 122, 131, 144
Eltham Palace 219

F

Fisher, John, Bishop 12, 33, 109, 215
Flanders Mare 19, 59, 164
Foxe, John 41, 91, 135, 240
Francis I, King 8, 102, 157, 205

G

Gardiner, Stephen 90
Gregory, Philippa 7, 10, 12, 13, 16, 33, 34, 46, 106, 108, 213

H

Harleston, Elizabeth 175
Henry II 107
Henry VII 24
Henry VIII 7, 9, 23, 34, 49, 53, 60, 83, 85, 102, 129, 132, 137, 141, 161, 202,
      211, 214
  Bigamy 157
Hever Castle 37, 122, 123, 189, 191, 192, 195, 197, 200, 201, 225
Holbein, Hans 48, 60, 61, 70, 116, 122
Horndon-on-the-Hill 125
Howard 9
  Catherine 19, 63, 64, 67, 107, 114, 116, 121, 123, 151, 171, 177
    Child Abuse 71
  Elizabeth 170, 201
Howard, Edward 70

J

Jean du Bellay 202
Jousting 132, 164

K

Kell Positive 129
Kingston, Sir William 110, 155, 163, 181, 220, 221, 237

L

Lefevre, Jean 215
Lisle, Lord Arthur 163
Lock, William 184
Louis VII 107

Luther 59, 62, 206

M

Madeleine of Valois 102
Manox, Henry 69, 70, 71, 72
Margaret of Austria 35, 42, 43
Margery Horsman 170
Mary Tudor 12, 60, 131, 155, 215
Melville-Jackson, George 96
Mont, Christopher 59
More, Sir Thomas 109, 191, 206, 221
Mouat, Dr. 5, 97, 113, 115, 116, 117, 121, 122, 123, 127

N

Neville, John 84, 86
Neville, Margaret 86
Norris, Sir Henry 97, 147, 149, 174, 176, 213, 219, 220, 231
Northlegh 202

O

Other Boleyn Girl, The 7, 8, 9, 10, 11, 12, 14, 15, 16, 33, 34, 35, 37, 38, 40, 41, 46, 106, 108, 147, 201, 239

P

Parker, Henry 207
Parker, Jane 10, 170, 207
Parker, Matthew 186
Parr, Catherine 19, 53, 83, 84, 85, 87, 212
Penshurst Place 189, 191, 192, 195, 196, 197, 202
Percy, Henry 8, 34, 40, 212
Pole, Margaret 97, 116, 117
Protestant 13, 34, 41, 43, 52, 62, 239

R

Reformation 19, 34, 35, 41, 43, 46, 106, 204, 239

S

Salle Church 124
Sander, Nicholas 3, 11, 34, 39, 46, 144

Savage, Anne 176
Scrope, Mary, Lady Kingston 172
Seymour, Edward 67, 116
Seymour, Jane 12, 19, 47, 86, 143, 164, 169, 173, 212
    Coronation 55
Seymour, Mary 85
Seymour, Thomas 14, 41, 52, 85, 87, 88, 89, 92, 178
Shelton, Lady Anne 172
Shelton, Madge 14, 174
Skip, John 187
Smeaton, Mark 97, 147, 215, 219, 220, 233
Smith, John 184
Stoner, Elizabeth 173
St Peter ad Vincula 5, 97, 113, 117, 121, 225, 234, 238

T

Talbot, Mary 8
Taylor, George 181
Thomas, Lord Burgh 183
Tudors, The, T.V. Show 17, 24, 67, 71, 76, 106, 143, 145, 213
Tunstall, Bishop 84

U

Uvedale, John 184

W

Waltham Abbey 202
Westminster Abbey 96, 98, 113, 158, 219, 220
Weston, Sir Francis 11, 97, 147, 219, 220, 232
Whitehall Palace 50, 53
Wingfield, Lady Bridget 174
Witch 12, 13, 19, 34, 39, 42, 95, 111, 125
Wolf Hall 47, 50
Wolsey, Cardinal 8, 12, 135, 169, 202, 207
Woodville, Elizabeth 105, 107
Wriothesley, Charles 12, 221
Wriothesley, Thomas 90
Wyatt, George 4, 136, 163, 169, 214
Wyatt, Sir Thomas 4, 124, 163

Visit Today

www.TheAnneBoleynFiles.com

The #1 site online for all things Tudor including:

- On this day in history
- Anne Boleyn Facts
- Tudor costumes and jewelry
- Book Reviews
- In depth research on the Boleyn family
- An incredibly active forum and discussion area
- Blog articles about all things Tudor
- A **FREE Report** on Anne Boleyn

Why not visit www.theanneboleynfiles.com today
to see what everyone has been talking about!

Exclusive
Members Website

http://members.theanneboleynfiles.com/

Made in the USA
Lexington, KY
20 May 2012